...AYS — Series

THE MERCHANT OF VENICE

William Shakespeare A3

Editors:
Linda Cookson A1
Bryan Loughrey A2

Longman Critical Essays

Editors: Linda Cookson and Bryan Loughrey

Titles in the series:

CONTENTS

PREFACE

Like all professional groups, literary critics have developed their own specialised language. This is not necessarily a bad thing. Sometimes complex concepts can only be described in a terminology far removed from everyday speech. Academic jargon, however, creates an unnecessary barrier between the critic and the intelligent but less practised reader.

This danger is particularly acute where scholarly books and articles are re-packaged for a student audience. Critical anthologies, for example, often contain extracts from longer studies originally written for specialists. Deprived of their original context, these passages can puzzle and at times mislead. The essays in this volume, however, are all specially commissioned, self-contained works, written with the needs of students firmly in mind.

This is not to say that the contributors — all experienced critics and teachers — have in any way attempted to simplify the complexity of the issues with which they deal. On the contrary, they explore the central problems of the text from a variety of critical perspectives, reaching conclusions which are challenging and at times mutually contradictory.

They try, however, to present their arguments in a direct, accessible language and to work within the limitations of scope and length which students inevitably face. For this reason, essays are generally rather briefer than is the practice; they address quite specific topics; and, in line with examination requirements, they incorporate precise textual detail into the body of the discussion.

They offer, therefore, working examples of the kind of essay-writing skills which students themselves are expected to develop. Their diversity, however, should act as a reminder that in the field of literary studies there is no such thing as a 'model' answer. Good essays are the outcome of a creative engagement with literature, of sensitive, attentive reading and careful thought. We hope that those contained in this volume will encourage students to return to the most important starting point of all, the text itself, with renewed excitement and the determination to explore more fully their own critical responses.

How to use this volume

Obviously enough, you should start by reading the text in question. The one assumption that all the contributors make is that you are already familiar with this. It would be helpful, of course, to have read further — perhaps other works by the same author or by influential contemporaries. But we don't assume that you have yet had the opportunity to do this and any references to historical background or to other works of literature are explained.

You should, perhaps, have a few things to hand. It is always a good idea to keep a copy of the text nearby when reading critical studies. You will almost certainly want to consult it when checking the context of quotations or pausing to consider the validity of the critic's interpretation. You should also try to have access to a good dictionary, and ideally a copy of a dictionary of literary terms as well. The contributors have tried to avoid jargon and to express themselves clearly and directly. But inevitably there will be occasional words or phrases with which you are unfamiliar. Finally, we would encourage you to make notes, summarising not just the argument of each essay but also your own responses to what you have read. So keep a pencil and notebook at the ready.

Suitably equipped, the best thing to do is simply begin with whichever topic most interests you. We have deliberately organised each volume so that the essays may be read in any order. One consequence of this is that, for the sake of clarity and self-containment, there is occasionally a degree of overlap between essays. But at least you are not forced to follow one — fairly arbitrary — reading sequence.

Each essay is followed by brief 'Afterthoughts', designed to highlight points of critical interest. But remember, these are only there to remind you that it is *your* responsibility to question what you read. The essays printed here are not a series of 'model' answers to be slavishly imitated and in no way should they be regarded as anything other than a guide or stimulus for your own thinking. We hope for a critically involved response: 'That was interesting. But if *I* were tackling the topic . . . !'

Read the essays in this spirit and you'll pick up many of the skills of critical composition in the process. We have, however, tried to provide more explicit advice in 'A practical guide to essay writing'. You may find this helpful, but do not imagine it offers any magic formulas. The quality of your essays ultimately depends on the quality of your engagement with literary texts. We hope this volume spurs you on to read these with greater understanding and to explore your responses in greater depth.

A note on the text

All references are to the New Penguin Shakespeare edition of *The Merchant of Venice*, ed. M Moelwyn Merchant.

John E Cunningham

John E Cunningham currently divides his time between writing and travel. He is the author of numerous critical studies.

ESSAY

Which is the Merchant here?

On those quiz games which seem to be the lifework of the daytime viewing public, from time to time the question is asked: 'Who *was* the Merchant of Venice?' Those of us who happen — quite accidentally — to be passing the set at the time smile, smug in our superior knowledge that the Merchant was Antonio; but the almost universal false reply contains a truth. In the modern consciousness of it, this play is 'about' Shylock, not about the man whose position gave it its title. Shylock is regarded by actors as the plum part, Portia follows a good second, the romantic lead Bassanio is a poor third, Antonio nowhere.

Besides the mere size of the part — Antonio has fewer than 200 of the play's 2,500 lines, many of them quite pedestrian at that — there are several other obvious reasons for this mistaken view of his unimportance. We have grown so hypersensitive to any trace of what can be called racism that there has grown up quite an industry in proving that Shakespeare could never have met an overtly practising Jew — since Jews were expelled with great savagery by Edward I and not allowed back into England until Cromwell — only those few who had ostensibly accepted Christianity; or in arguing that he showed a far more tolerant attitude to racial divisions than did most of his fellows; or in suggesting that the play is a cleverly disguised satire on the Christians who hypocritically use the law to trip Shylock up and then force him to accept the faith he so potently abhorred in order to save his skin. The fortunes of Shylock's role — for quite a long period played simply for comedy, a pantomime villain — are certainly interesting, but it is easy to forget, in the drama of the great trial scene where he is opposed to Portia, that for the greater part of the play Shylock the usurer is set against the liberal merchant, Antonio. Nor does the importance of Antonio's role readily appear even in the closing scene — almost his last words are 'I am dumb!', as well he might be when he is told something so impossible as that his fortunes are all restored — and throughout the matrimonial squabbles of the episode he seems something of an odd man out. Gratiano's concluding bawdy pun about marriage is not for him.

But Antonio begins the play — for it is to him that the opening words are given — on a quite different note from its ending. He talks about his 'sadness', a word implying sobriety rather than misery, in what seems to be an apology to his friends. From their frivolity and his own status as a merchant it seems he is older than they. From the joking suggestion that he might be in love we also infer that he is unmarried and so without heirs. Regretting his own inability to be as light-hearted as his companions, he says:

> In sooth I know not why I am so sad.
> It wearies me, you say it wearies you;
> But how I caught it, found it, or came by it,
> What stuff 'tis made of, whereof it is born,
> I am to learn

(I.1.1–5)

This speech achieves more than appears at first. It sets up the plot, for we do learn, a little later, the immediate reason for his sombre mood, when he asks Bassanio to give him more information about the lady 'To whom you swore a secret pilgrimage' (I.1.119–120). It also sets up the character of the speaker. Of the four temperaments then generally recognised — choleric, phlegmatic, sanguine and melancholy — Antonio, like Romeo and Hamlet, belongs to the last. It was typical of melancholy, which we might call cyclic depression, that it had no obvious cause. Antonio simply accepts his own temperament and the sort of life which it makes him lead:

> I hold the world but as the world, Gratiano,
> A stage where every man must play a part,
> And mine a sad one.

(I.1.77–79)

This same resignation to his lot — an almost apathetic pessimism — is maintained much later in the play, when it seems he cannot escape the penalty of the bond:

> I am a tainted wether of the flock,
> Meetest for death. The weakest kind of fruit
> Drops earliest to the ground, and so let me.

(IV.1.114–116)

Why he should so regard himself as particularly expendable is not at all clear; but at least one famous melancholy hero in Shakespeare found the thought of suicide attractive at times, and Antonio seems less disposed to struggle for his life than do his friends on his behalf.

If there were no more to him than this — a sober, negative, almost-failed businessman — then the play is indeed badly out of balance and Shylock should walk off with it, as many people think he does. Though the twentieth century is pregnant with stories of failure on the stock exchange, it is perhaps hard for us to realise how well the first audiences would have responded to the deep insecurity of Antonio's way of life. So perilous were long sea voyages held to be that speculators would pay twenty per cent on money left with them by travellers, recouping amply from the wealth of those who failed to return: a measure of risk mentioned in Shakespeare's last play, *The Tempest*. Fortunes were made and lost in the City in England's expanding mercantile and maritime economy — the parallel with Venice was close. So when Solanio says:

> Believe me, sir, had I such venture forth,
> The better part of my affections would
> Be with my hopes abroad

(I.1.15–17)

we need not suppose he is joking. Only ten years before these lines were written, the naval might of Spain had been beaten as much by the weather as by Drake. Drake himself returned from one expedition with two out of three ships lost; Hawkins once brought back fifteen men of a crew of a hundred. The anxious side of Antonio's nature is well founded.

If the insecurity of his wealth is properly and early established, it is also quickly shown that his melancholy is not only an arbitrary trait of character. In the latter part of the first scene we are shown that he had prior knowledge of his friend's intention to seek his fortune elsewhere with a lady. In a speech ostensibly self-deprecating, Bassanio reveals much about their relationship:

> ... but my chief care
> Is to come fairly off from the great debts
> Wherein my time, something too prodigal,
> Hath left me gaged. To you Antonio,
> I owe the most in money and in love,
> And from your love I have a warranty
> To unburden all my plots and purposes

(I.1.127–133)

Antonio has been enormously indulgent towards him — a fond father, perhaps, with a surrogate son — and money is something to be treated on the whole lightly.

In an age when a pair of shoes can hardly inhabit the same box without being accused of unnatural vice, it is inevitable that some readers and commentators should suppose that the friendship between these two men, the one older, the other obviously attractive, the generosity one-way, should be homosexual: this is to comment on our own age rather than to throw light on Shakespeare's. He held, with a long line of thinkers before him, going back to Plato at least, that friendship was the noblest form of love since it asked nothing but to be itself; in a sexual relationship pleasure is given and received. In his neo-platonic age the debate between the rival claims of love and friendship was a popular intellectual exercise. When Lorenzo opens a scene by saying abruptly:

> Madam, although I speak it in your presence,

> You have a noble and a true conceit
> Of godlike amity, which appears most strongly
> In bearing thus the absence of your lord
>
> (III.4.1–4)

a modern audience supposes that he is commenting on the fact that Portia is not biting her nails or punishing the sack-bottle in her husband's frustrating absence. Earlier hearers would pick up the 'true conceit of godlike amity' as a reference to the love-friendship debate in which, we presume, the two have been engaging: Lorenzo says that Portia has a true understanding of the lofty, spiritual nature of friendship — her 'nobility' would appear in her not being jealous of her husband's affection for Antonio.

It is important for us to understand this, not only to make sense of Antonio's attachment, but to help us evaluate Bassanio too. Such love between men was and is of its very nature unselfish: it depends on reciprocal generosity. Bassanio is not abusing it when he asks his friend to lend him more money on top of that which is already owed: that is the proper office of a friend. In his turn, when he has means at his disposal, he is ready to put everything aside, most notably his own desires, to fly to his friend and offer whatever he can in comfort and aid. Antonio best expresses this element of their friendship — and of his own unselfish character — in a speech which has to be read for him: his letter of appeal:

> And since in paying it [the bond], it is impossible I should live, all debts are cleared between you and I if I might but see you at my death. Notwithstanding, use your pleasure. If your love do not persuade you to come, let not my letter.
>
> (III.2.317–321)

This same generosity of spirit towards Bassanio is repeated when he stands on the very brink of death:

> Commend me to your honourable wife,
> Tell her the process of Antonio's end,
> Say how I loved you, speak me fair in death,
> And when the tale is told, bid her be judge
> Whether Bassanio had not once a love.

Repent but you that you shall lose your friend,
And he repents not that he pays your debt

(IV.1.270–276)

and he ends with a grim pun, a last attempt by a man not noted for a sense of humour, to cheer someone up.

A generous friend, then: what sort of an enemy is Antonio? For we must not lose sight of the fact that his most important function in the play is as the object of Shylock's hatred. Those anxious to read the story as a statement about racism do not lack for material. In a speech of some force, Shylock accuses Antonio of public insult and worse for his money-lending:

You call me misbeliever, cut-throat dog,
And spit upon my Jewish gaberdine,
And all for use of that which is mine own.

(I.3.108–110)

Antonio replies, hotly agreeing:

I am as like to call thee so again,
To spit on thee again, to spurn thee too

(I.3.127–128)

— made more insulting to contemporary ears by the use of the singular form 'thee', where Shylock uses the plural. Such an overt hatred not only for Shylock's practices but for his race is offensive to us, but would not be to the original audiences, familiar with tales of fearsome extortions exacted by money-lenders and thinking of the Jews as a race accursed: though Shakespeare here and elsewhere gives them a sharp taste of what it is actually like to be so esteemed. But in any case the speech and our possible reactions to it have been pre-empted by Shylock himself in an earlier aside. As Antonio enters — his essentially kindly nature already well established in the opening scene — Shylock says:

How like a fawning publican he looks.
I hate him for he is a Christian;
But more, for that in low simplicity
He lends out money gratis and brings down
The rate of usance here with us in Venice.

(I.3.38–42)

Thus a perfect antithesis is presented to us. He hates Antonio for what he is and for what he does: in just the same way, Antonio hates him.

This contrast is continued in the discussion of the morality of usury which follows; a discussion which does not appear in any of Shakespeare's likely sources. The justification which Shylock offers is from the Old Testament, the Book of Genesis. Antonio dismisses it to his friend by saying that 'The devil can cite Scripture for his purpose' (I.3.95). But the two men display a totally different attitude to money — and some critics believe that money is the sub-text of the whole play. To Antonio it is a means to help a friend to happiness, something of no value in itself: to Shylock it is a way of life and a means to power, more important to him — 'Would she were hearsed at my foot, and the ducats in her coffin!' (III.1.81–82) — than his own daughter.

Antonio's anger with Shylock and his round dismissal of Shylock's whole view of life make it hard in the theatre for us to accept the way in which he almost immediately falls in with the terms of the bond, proposed as a joke: one which Bassanio certainly does not like. Perhaps it is a part of the generosity of spirit that we have seen in the merchant that he is prepared to suppose an equal 'kindness' in others, even in someone so unlikely.

Generosity to his enemies is certainly something of which he is capable, in strong contrast with Shylock. When the bond falls due, and Shylock's hatred is exacerbated by his daughter's desertion to what he sees as Antonio's camp, the Jew is pitiless. Offered every inducement to relent, he refuses and is then trapped by an application of his own values.

In this, so much attention is centred on the court duel between him and Portia that the man at the heart of the issue is almost overlooked. When the Duke remits the sentence of death but pronounces the whole of Shylock's wealth to be forfeit — half to Antonio, half to the state, the latter to be commuted to a fine if Shylock will humble himself to ask it — it is to Antonio that Portia properly turns to ask what mercy *he* can offer to the man who a moment before had refused any to him. Antonio replies:

> So please my lord the Duke and all the court
> To quit the fine for one half of his goods,

> I am content, so he will let me have
> The other half in use

(IV.1.377–380)

The wording is ambiguous, but must mean either that he is ready to let the half due to the state be altogether waived, or that he readily agrees with the suggestion that it be commuted merely to a fine: either way Shylock will retain a substantial capital. The other terms on which he insists — that Shylock should leave all he has at death to his daughter and new son-in-law, and should himself immediately accept Christianity — have been much misunderstood by modern readers and spectators; but in contemporary terms they are proper and generous. His daughter, his only child, would expect to inherit; he himself would have no hope of heaven if he remained a Jew. Antonio wishes, without prompting, to save his deadly enemy from poverty in this world and damnation in the next — that is how the action would then have been construed: it is much more than mercy.

But since Shakespeare has been at such pains to show how intensely Shylock's faith is part of his life, his enforced conversion is not something we could contemplate without unease, and he is briskly removed from the scene as soon as he has agreed to the terms.

It has often been remarked that the verbal music, moonlight, reunions of lovers and comedy of the rings in the last Act are a necessary means of lightening the atmosphere after the trial: Antonio's role, as underestimated in this part of the play as elsewhere, appears to be twofold.

When the teasing of Bassanio and Gratiano becomes too distressing, it is he who reminds them — and us, perhaps — of the serious side of the story:

> I once did lend my body for his wealth,
> Which but for him that had your husband's ring
> Had quite miscarried.

(V.1.249–251)

And it is he who is the reconciler, he whom Portia symbolically asks to return the ring to its proper wearer.

Reconciled, then, and happy in one another, they pass into

the house. The Merchant is no longer in Venice, that city of deals and deviousness, but in Belmont, which is always a place of happiness and high spirits — except, perhaps, for the disappointed suitors, and their scenes end cheerfully enough. Supremely, in a play so much concerned with money, it is a place where wealth is important only for the happiness it can bring, the release of a friend from bondage — pay treble, it does not matter, says Portia — the security of a young couple for the future, something to be given away, not 'lent as to an enemy' as it was in Venice. Antonio, a man who has made his living in an uncertain world of international trade, but who is as generous to foe as to friend, acts as some sort of bridge between the two worlds of Venice and Belmont.

What happens then is, of course, no concern of the dramatist and should be none of ours: whether we suppose that Antonio stayed with his friends or went back to the commercial world in which his credit has been so remarkably restored; but in the theatre the other characters leave the stage, as is right, in pairs, as they will live thereafter. Antonio is still the odd man out that he was at the play's beginning, a grave reminder of other worlds than Belmont: as lonely in his way, perhaps, as Shylock. But where Shylock has renounced his daughter, always unhappy under his roof — 'Our house is hell' she had said feelingly — and is hated by all, Antonio is rich in friends, and has secured the happiness not only of the man who perhaps represented a son to him, but also of the daughter that her true father had rejected. This merchant has traded in a good deal more than can be quoted on the market.

AFTERTHOUGHTS

1

Which part would *you* choose to play in *The Merchant of Venice*?

2

Discuss the differing views of Cunningham (pages 12–13) and Holderness (page 36) on the nature of Antonio's relationship with Bassanio. With which, if either, of these views do you agree?

3

Do you accept that Antonio's terms for Shylock's freedom are 'proper and generous' (page 16)?

4

Can it ever be useful to speculate 'What happens then?' (page 17) at the end of a play?

Charles Moseley

*Charles Moseley teaches English at
Cambridge University and at the Leys
School, Cambridge. He is the author of
numerous critical studies.*

ESSAY

Portia's music and the naughty world

Any Renaissance household of consequence (as Portia's obviously
is) would include a small group of professional musicians: the
'music . . . of the house' (V.1.98). They provided music, vocal or
instrumental or both, for the ceremonies and the enjoyments of
daily life as well as for special occasions. So in *The Merchant of
Venice* (or *Much Ado About Nothing*, where Leonato employs a
solo singer and a group who play for the two dances) Shakespeare
presents a believable picture of noble society; but his use of
music and musicians is not simply explicable as a bit of everyday realism. While his theatre company included singers and
musicians who would be annoyed if a job for them was not quite
often written into the plays, music signified far more to his
audience than it does to us. We need to examine this background
briefly before we can grasp the significance of Portia's music.

Shakespeare's life coincided with a remarkable period in
English music. Visiting foreigners commented on the excellence
of even amateur performers, and it would be nothing unusual for
tavern customers during a convivial evening to call for the
songbooks and sightread in multi-part harmony. Practical skill
was balanced surprisingly far down the social scale by at least

19

some theoretical understanding: references and allusions in popular literature, including plays, show that audiences were expected to know much more of the theory of music than we might think. For while audiences certainly demanded entertainment from plays, they also expected to look beneath the surface story. They expected the play's structure, the nature and recognised 'types' of its characters, its frame of image references, and its staging, to point watchers to the deeper levels of meaning. The use — or not — of music is an important part of the symbolic design of a play.

The theatre building was itself a well-used symbol of the world. In it, the musicians were often positioned above 'The Heavens', the canopy painted with the Zodiac that most authorities maintain covered the stage. For music was, literally, heavenly: the turning concentric spheres of the universe, as Lorenzo explains to Jessica, were alive, the in-dwelling spirits of each uttering single notes which combined to form the holy and healing Music of the Spheres that Pericles thinks he hears. (This ancient idea goes back beyond Plato to Pythagoras, but had been thoroughly Christianised by, among others, St Augustine and Boethius.) But that everlasting music of perfection is inaudible on earth not just because man is a spirit clothed in the changeable 'muddy vesture of decay' (V.1.64), but because of the breach in the Chain of Being resulting from Adam's primal sin. Sin destroyed the answering harmony in man, and the more evilly disposed a man is, the less music is in him (V.1.83ff) — like Shylock (II.5.30) or Cassius (*Julius Caesar*, I.2.204). Nevertheless, imperfect human music recalls its heavenly original; the Florentine philosopher Marsilio Ficino argued that human souls loved music because it reminded them of the divine music, and that it had a capacity to heal, to call order out of disorder, to affect mind and behaviour powerfully. Those effects were much studied. Ficino (and Lorenzo in V.1.70ff) are echoed by Robert Burton — no original thinker — in his *Anatomy of Melancholy* (1621): music 'ravisheth the soul, *regina sensuum*, the queen of the senses', by 'sweet pleasure'.[1] It can cure melancholy and madness, and lead to love. The modes had different effects,

---

[1] Part 2, Sect. 2, Memb. 6, Subsect. 3.

which we can be sure Portia, briefing her music before Bassanio chooses, knew about: the Dorian 'giveth wisdom and chastity'; the Phrygian 'stirreth to battle and inflameth the desire of fury'; the Aeolian 'appeaseth the tempests of the mind and bringeth in sleep'; the Lydian 'quickeneth understanding in them that be dull, and induceth appetite of celestial things'.[2] Burton calls music 'divine' (immediately noting *'numen inest numeris'* — 'there is a spiritual power in numbers and rhythm'), and reminds us of poet/musicians like Arion, Orpheus and Hercules, who civilised, created and vivified by their art. According to myth the walls of Thebes were sung into being; King David, the Type of the Christian Prince and ancestor of Christ himself, was always represented as a poet and harpist. Many who watched *The Merchant of Venice* when it was new would recall that in France in the darkening months before the Wars of Religion broke out, there had been a serious attempt, through an Academy of Poetry and Music, to bring Catholic and Protestant together to make music which would reconcile them and remove the will to fight. Milton's *At a Solemn Music* summarises these ideas succinctly: music and poetry present to the 'phantasie . . . That undisturbed Song of pure content/ Ay sung before the sapphire-colour'd throne . . . Where the bright Seraphim in burning row/ Their loud up-lifted Angel trumpets blow.' Hearing it clearly could make us 'on Earth with undiscording voice/ . . . rightly answer . . . As once we did, till disproportion'd sin/ Jarr'd against natures chime, and with harsh din/ Broke the fair musick that all creatures made.'

It is this common idea of music — healing, transcendent, mystical, mathematical — that lies behind Shakespeare using it to heal Lear's mind or to summon Hermione (in *The Winter's Tale*) back to life in Leontes' wiser arms. The musical concord of the spheres, each occupying its proper place or degree, is a metaphor for order in state, in family, in heaven, in the mind. In *Troilus and Cressida* Act I scene 3 Ulysses uses a musical conceit to warn of the dangers of disorder: our word 'discord', now used almost always in common speech without its musical

---

[2] *The autobiography of Thomas Whythorne*, ed. J M Osborne (New York and Toronto, 1962).

sense, once had *only* a musical sense. And, finally, for Shakeapeare music is a way of defining happy human love. In Sonnet 8 'the true concord of well-tuned sounds' mirrors harmonious human love, for:

> Mark how one string, sweet husband to another,
> Strikes each in each by mutual ordering;
> Resembling sire and child and happy mother,
> Who, all in one, one pleasing note do sing.

When he wants us to evaluate the love between Bassanio and Portia and between Jessica and Lorenzo, and when he wants to point through the human relationship to some of the moral and philosophical concerns of the play, he uses musical means to do it.

It is arresting that this play, where Shakespeare discusses music more fully (in V.1.53ff) than in any other, hardly mentions it — even in the imagery — except at two critical moments: the winning of Portia, and then when the storms that nearly wrecked Antonio's and Bassanio's venture are over and Portia returns to the home where she is reunited to 'the semblance of [her] soul' (III.4.20). At these moments, however, music continues for some time, and rather longer than is usual elsewhere: in III.2 it supports a minimum of twenty-three lines, twelve of them sung (probably with elaborate divisions), and could usefully be maintained for a further thirty-two lines while Bassanio continues his musing until making his choice. In V.1 the musicians are summoned at line 53, and for thirty-four slow lines Lorenzo gives Jessica some elementary instruction in what her father, who was deaf to music and blind to Christian Grace, never told her. The musicians start to play at line 68; 'Mark the music' (line 88) suggests that there is a substantial musical passage before Portia and Nerissa enter; the musicians play on till line 109, while Portia and Nerissa see the light shining in the darkness, and engage in musing talk that looks beneath the surface of things, even playfully seeing the two human lovers before them as divine (the moon) and human (Endymion) united. These two passages have complex significance, and of both Portia is the ultimate focus.

So, first of all, we must consider her. She is, after all, the prize of this test of the caskets, the patron of the 'music', and in

V.1 the elaborate discussion of cosmic harmony and earthly disharmony is a prelude to her entrance. She is explicitly linked to the 'touches of sweet harmony' (V.1.56ff): she is won to music, is 'draw[n] . . . home with music' (V.1.68). No one would wish to play down the individuality Shakespeare has given her: witty, resourceful, amusing, authoritative, she was clearly attracted to Bassanio on first seeing him (I.2.114), and before his choice he and she, using all the conventional imagery of love poetry, play an elaborate Game of Love (III.2.1–62) which is wholly charming — and, on stage, naturalistic and credible. Yet she is clearly symbolic too. When we first hear of her she is something for which much must be ventured and risked (I.1.161ff), just as Antonio risks his riches on the unstable seas of fortune. Even so, Bassanio's description of her to Antonio passes quickly over her wealth to stress her moral qualities. Moreover, she lives in the strangely named Belmont — the 'Hill Beautiful' — like any heroine of chivalric romance who must be won by a test or ordeal (which is explicitly how she sees herself, III.2.57). She is constantly associated with the Quest of the Golden Fleece (I.1.170–172; cf. III.2.241), which Renaissance scholars usually interpreted as symbolic of man's quest for Wisdom. Wisdom, and its capacity to see through Law and Justice to Mercy, is certainly what some would argue Portia shows in her descent from her mountain to the commercial, bond-ridden world of Venice, whence she rescues Antonio. Wisdom is certainly the quality Renaissance moralists felt young people should seek, and be encouraged and supported in that search by those who called themselves their true friends. A symbolical reading of the play, which Shakespeare seems to offer us in the trial scene, in the behaviour of Jessica, and in the winning of Portia, might thus suggest that we should see the marriage of Portia and Bassanio as a study of the goals of friendship, the completing of an education begun in love and generosity by the winning of wisdom and the harmonising of male and female, as two halves of a whole, in a symbolic marriage. But because of the tense sincerity and wit of their verbal exchanges before the choice, we can believe their love to be genuinely passionate while still accepting its symbolic importance. This marriage is a treasure won by venturing the trial of the caskets as a merchant ventures his ships on the sea (II.1.34); and Fortune, since 'hanging and wiving go by destiny' (II.9.83), has confirmed what is right and just, the true order: '[you] will no doubt never be chosen by any rightly but one who you shall rightly love' (I.2.30–31).

Wisdom as a prize would sit ill with either of Bassanio's two predecessors in the ritual. Morocco has real dignity, real import-ance, and a not unattractive confidence in his own worth and powers. Yet his choice confirms that this confidence in his own deserts lacks wisdom — 'Had you been as wise as bold' (II.7.70) — it presupposes that the world must be as he sees it, without obscurity, deception, or the vagaries of chance and Fortune. His marrying Portia would not be a closing of a gap in creation. Arragon is a simple fool, puffed up with silly pride of birth and rank, whose fittest reward is the portrait of a blinking idiot — just as the death's head reminded Morocco of the limit of those powers and qualities of which he was so proud. Now, apart from the flourish of cornets — mere Renaissance good manners to people of high rank — before the entries of these two, these scenes are wholly without music: there could be no harmony in such marriages, for to win wisdom a man 'must give and hazard all he hath' (II.9.21), as Antonio did for Bassanio, and only the person who sees beneath the outward show (III.2.73–74) is capable of wisdom.

Bassanio's choice, by contrast, is preceded by and ac-complished to music. Portia may hope that, if he is the man she thinks he is, the music will put him into the right frame of mind for wise choice. It does indeed make him reflective and quiet, talking, unlike Arragon and Morocco, 'to himself' rather than to those who watch. (The stage direction at III.2.62, certainly records early playhouse practice and may be Shakespeare's own.)[3]

The music suggests to Portia a pair of elaborate conceits. A Bassanio who failed would be like the swan (III.2.44), which,

---

[3] In the source, Ser Giovanni's *Il Pecorone*, the eventually successful Gianetto is given a hint that enables him to win the lady, and some have seen the song as doing as much for Bassanio: certainly three of its lines rhyme with 'lead'. But Portia has said explicitly that she will not help Bassanio (lines 11–12), and implicitly that she would abide by the scheme set up by her father (I.2.20ff), and was reproved by Nerissa for even chafing at it: it is quite out of character for her to cheat in a ritual of this importance.

mute in life, was supposed to sing as it died. But that idea is dismissed as soon as the thought of tears and replaced by swelling conceits of triumphal, festive music: the monarch acclaimed on his coronation day, or the bridegroom soon to be monarch of his lady's 'New Found Land', as Donne put it. Portia is thinking of her own hoped-for marriage; but the husband and wife are an image of, and express something of the nature of, the prince wedded to his country. And the song itself warns Bassanio not to confuse real love with what we often mistake for it, 'Which alters when it alteration finds' (Sonnet 116), mere fancy begotten by the eyes.

What pulls all these ideas together is the reference to Hercules (III.2.55), for Portia casts herself as a new Hesione, to be won or rescued by the prowess of Hercules. The story of Hercules in the Renaissance was interpreted as a symbol of man's search for Wisdom, culminating in the test when Hercules has to choose between Pleasure and Virtue, and then find out how to reconcile them. Wisdom, once found, allows Hercules to be a benefactor of mankind, a founder of cities, a patron of the arts. Bassanio's successful choice shows he understands the need to see beneath the surface, to 'choose not by the view' — ironic when we recall that he will not recognise Portia disguised as a lawyer. The upshot is immediate marriage — the giving of a ring before witnesses (line 171) — and it is impossible not to see that marriage as carrying symbolic force. Bassanio is invested with control of Portia's property: Gratiano's image in line 241 suggests, to him, a successful commercial venture and, to us, the winning of wisdom, a growing up to full maturity, a 'find[ing of] the joys of heaven here on earth' (III.5.71), as Jessica says.

But those joys can only be glimpsed — through the eye of wisdom, through virtuous and wise love, through music. No sooner has the exalted union of Bassanio and Portia been highlighted by the much more earthy union of Nerissa and Gratiano than news of Antonio's plight separates the lovers. The momentary completeness has to be suspended because of the demands of the world of Venice: the vision of Truth and Beauty and Goodness may not be fully known while the lower world has its claims on man. So the circle of venturing continues. As Antonio ventured for Bassanio, and selflessly ventured Bassanio for Bassanio's own good knowing that he might lose the intimacy of his friendship when he was married, Portia ventures Bassanio to win Antonio from trouble, loving Antonio before she meets him (III.4.10–21; cf. 'Since you are dear bought, I will love you dear III.2.313).[4]

For this is what Lorenzo, whom Portia recognises as wise enough to have Belmont entrusted to him (III.4.25), is implying: we may know of, even hear hints of — 'mark the music' — the music of the spheres, but we cannot know it while on this earth. We can only imitate it as near as we can with our own music and in wise human love. Human beings live in a fallen world, subject to decay and mutability and sin, where Justice is necessary to regulate the affairs of men.

Portia and Nerissa too hear the music, of course. Nerissa simply recognises it as 'the music of the house' — she is as prosaic as her lover Gratiano. Portia, on the other hand, who thinks as symbolically and metaphorically here as she does in the casket scene, muses first on the little candle that would not be noticed in a room full of light, but which is striking when all else is dark: the power of goodness over evil. Then she hears her own music in a way she has not heard it before — it is 'sweeter than by day' — and points out how our valuation and understanding of things is so often dependent on circumstance and point of view. The idea can hardly not be self-referential in a play that presents us with enigmas and choices, and, perhaps, Portia offers us a way of valuing Bassanio's perception 'by season' (V.1.107) in the casket scene.

The transmission, similar to the stars raining down influence, of the wisdom and harmony of heaven to a lower world, could be seen as a parallel to the way Shakespeare links Belmont to the very different atmosphere in Venice. Here is a naughty world of trickery and revenge, of bonds and debt and punishment, where both Christian and Jew come off very badly. The play seems to be much concerned with knowing when to speak a word in season, with healing, with completing, with hazarding all in order to win true fulfilment; it is a play about generous

---

[4] Jessica, it could be argued, ventures for her love, and is accepted into the enchanted world of Belmont (III.2.237): Shylock loses his venturing because there is no love in him, not even for his daughter.

love, and about what the inability to give such love does to people. The love between Antonio and Bassanio is a textbook example of what Renaissance philosophers would have understood by Friendship, where the Friend seeks the ultimate, fulfilling, moral and spiritual good of the Beloved even if it involves his own loss of him. The clearly sexual as well as intellectual love between Portia and Bassanio is an image of cosmic and political harmony, highlighted by Lorenzo's love which rescues Jessica from a house that is 'Hell', and counterpointed by the much more obviously earthy (but nonetheless attractive) love of Gratiano and Nerissa. That sexual love, with the debt owed to a Friend's love, draws Portia from the enchanted mountain and engages her in the world of Venice: virtue, to be virtue, has to express itself in virtuous action. But in that world she cannot be recognised as herself, just as human music reminds us of but is not cosmic music. In Venice her first imperative is the need to engender mercy as well as to act justly; and when Shylock refuses that noble way forward, her wisdom allows her to free Antonio by using the very stipulations and legal demands of an enemy who will not accept grace and reconciliation when it is offered him. Antonio put his own life at risk to send Bassanio on a quest that might have lost him his society and love for ever, and for that generous act of Friendship he is taken up into the harmonious world of Belmont where his Friend will be lord in a symbolic happy marriage. It is Portia's wisdom, the goal of Bassanio's Quest, that saves Antonio. Portia's virtue and wisdom, once won by Bassanio, can then engage in the active and crude world where trade has to carry on, laws have to be made, and justice executed.

The magic, illusory, world of the theatre, where we feel real emotions in real time for imaginary people and events, is nothing if not moral: all Renaissance critics were agreed that drama is far more important morally, socially and politically than any mere story it may tell. It is, in fact, our Belmont. From it we need to learn, and to put those lessons into practice in our own Venice, to seek to transmit something of the harmony we glimpse into the naughty world.

AFTERTHOUGHTS

1

Explain the importance to this essay of the historical background given on pages 19–22. Could the significance of music in the play be understood without it?

2

Are you convinced that Portia's song should not be seen as helping Bassanio in his choice of casket (page 24, footnote)?

3

Do you agree with Moseley's view of the symbolic importance of Portia, as detailed in this essay?

4

Do you agree that drama is 'nothing if not moral' (page 27)?

Graham Holderness

Graham Holderness is Head of the Drama Department at Roehampton Institute, and has published numerous works of criticism.

ESSAY

Purse and person: for love or money

The Merchant of Venice is a comedy. As such it appears to be shaped by a dominant pattern of ultimate reconciliation, harmonising, unifying, balance. The comic pattern concludes by reconciling all contradictions, resolving all disharmonies, drawing all discordant elements into a unitary synthesis and integration. At the end of the play, this pattern is effected by various dramatic and poetic means: the symbolic harmony of marriage (there are four of them, already solemnised but still unconsummated); the reconciliation of disagreement (the dispute over the rings is a practical joke, a staged quarrel deliberately faked so as to restore subsequent unanimity); the clarification of deception and misunderstanding, especially the throwing off of disguise; and the symbolic harmony of music, familiarly acknowledged as the physical embodiment, in Elizabethan drama, of psychological and social concord. Lorenzo's set-piece speech on the music of the spheres unites all these levels of concord into a complex but unitary synthesis:

> Here will we sit and let the sounds of music
> Creep in our ears; soft stillness and the night
> Become the touches of sweet harmony.

Sit, Jessica. Look how the floor of heaven
Is thick inlaid with patens of bright gold.
There's not the smallest orb which thou beholdest
But in his motion like an angel sings,
Still choiring to the young-eyed cherubins;
Such harmony is in immortal souls

(V.I.55–63)

The speech formally links the idea of harmony in music with its demonstration given in the stage direction '*Music*', the peaceful 'paten' of nature with the unanimity of achieved relationship, the integrity of the soul with the elemental music of the spheres. On stage, musicians herald the return of Portia, whose successfully achieved quest prefigures unity and reconciliation among the play's dominant Christian community.

How perfect in fact is this harmony? are there no jarring notes, no false strings? does the comic pattern succeed in governing into integration all the discordant elements it strives to contain? or are there elements in the play which resist integration, defy reconciliation, refuse to be synthesised into the general comic perspective? To propose a suggestive comparison, *Twelfth Night* is known as one of the most serene and beautiful of Shakespeare's comedies: but as that play draws to its resolution, a shadow is cast across its theatrical concordat by the rejection of Malvolio. Like Shylock, Malvolio is perhaps a man more sinning than sinned against; but the play allows us at least the possibility of regarding him as a victim of persecution. He is a fool: but is he less ridiculous than the fashionably melancholy egotist Orsino? Is it natural justice that self-absorbed folly in a duke should reap such rich reward, while narcissistic blindness in a steward deserves ridicule and humiliation? Olivia certainly agrees that Malvolio has been 'notoriously abused'. In the conclusion to *Twelfth Night* we are aware that the harmonising and reconciliation of contradictions exact a certain price: that someone has to suffer by exclusion from what would otherwise be a perfect unity. Malvolio's exit casts a shadow over the play's conclusion.

It would be wrong to over-emphasise this detail. But it must at least force the possibility of glimpsing what is, from the perspective of the dominant group of characters, a harmonious and optimistic perspective, from another point of view: that of the alienated and excluded outsider. To Malvolio, the play's ending is tragic. If we refuse to accept the validity of that perspective, if we dissociate our emotions from Malvolio's tragedy, then while we are accepting the comic pattern as dominant, we are surely declining to hear a particularly poignant strain in the play's poetic music. We watch Malvolio rushing off stage, shouting his absurd threat of vengeance ('I'll be revenged on the whole pack of you!'), and respond with a laughter which, though not uncompromised by guilt and anxiety, depends on a commitment to the comic reconciliation of the Illyrian court. In another play by Shakespeare we witness the spectacle of an old man who has acted foolishly, who has also suffered from the curse of self-love, rushing out into a storm, shouting a very similar imprecation of revenge, wrung from the agony of impotence: 'I will do such things . . .'. There in *King Lear* the perspective is unmistakably tragic, because the dramatic structure inclines us to view the situation from the point of view of the excluded, rather than from the perspective of those who, for whatever reasons, exclude.

This is not an attempt to revalue *Twelfth Night* as a tragedy: it is rather to insist on the tragic potentiality of some of its elements. We don't take Malvolio's revenge seriously, because we are assured of the benevolent and beneficial power of the harmonised court. The closer we draw to Malvolio's own situation, the clearer our perception of him as a victim of persecution, the more valid and threatening becomes his demand for revenge. Which brings us back to Shylock. Both Malvolio and Shylock are members of a minority group within their respective societies: a Puritan and a Jew. In history such minorities have been cruelly persecuted and oppressed: but each too has had its moments of triumph or acceptance. Malvolio's revenge on the carefree and irresponsible aristocracy took concrete form not long after Shakespeare's death, with the Civil War and the execution of a king. In 1655 Oliver Cromwell, leader of the organised Malvolios, re-admitted the Jews to England for the first time since their banishment in 1209. As commercial production and exchange became in the course of England's 'bourgeois revolution' more dependent on a money economy, requiring the free flow of credit and finance, Malvolio found in Shylock an indispensable ally.

The discordant elements of *The Merchant of Venice* centre on Shylock, and extend from this central figure across other areas of the play. It is the peculiarly intractable nature of the play's discords which accounts for the remarkable stage-history of *The Merchant*, a history containing some extraordinary transformations. In terms of standard Elizabethan attitudes and conventions, Shylock can be assimilated to a definite convention, that of the stage Jew, a variant of the medieval dramatic Vice, embellished with the trappings of contemporary anti-semitism and the uniform of grotesque farce (red wigs and huge painted noses). It has often been argued that we should try to read and view Elizabethan plays in the context of Elizabethan attitudes and prejudices, avoiding the imposition of our own more tolerant and liberal values. It is however clearly impossible to read a play about the persecution of a Jew with disinterested historical objectivity: relatively recent events such as the Holocaust, a modern tragedy which seemed to confirm very ancient legends of racial persecution, render such an operation of historical distancing out of the question. The kind of cruel amusement which the educated Elizabethan could evidently direct towards Jews can hardly be revived in a culture where the names of those Second World War concentration camps in which six million were annihilated — Auschwitz, Dachau, Belsen — carry such potent symbolic force.

On the other hand, as much recent criticism has convincingly shown, we cannot always be quite so sure as scholars once were of exactly how such 'standard' ideas and prejudices were held by Elizabethan audiences; nor can we confidently attribute those orthodox opinions to Shakespeare or to the plays he wrote. The reading of an Elizabethan play involves both an act of historical imagination, the act of thinking and feeling one's way into a very different historical culture; and an awareness of the ways in which subsequent historical developments and modern beliefs may have changed the play's possibilities of interpretation. Reading in this dialectical way, it becomes possible to recognise within an Elizabethan play potentialities which become fully articulate only in modern interpretation. The modern recognition of Shylock as a tragic figure, which is so incompatible with that Elizabethan grotesque with the red wig and the artificial nose, may be a recognition of possibilities historically inscribed into the play.

The tendency to see Shylock not as a comic villain, but as something closer to a hero or hero-manqué, began much earlier than the twentieth century's experience of fascism. As early as the eighteenth century the role was treated with some measure of tragic dignity. And in the course of the romantic movement of the early nineteenth century a serious revaluation and reinterpretation of Shylock appeared on both critical and theatrical agendas. Edmund Kean performed Shylock in 1814 as a tragic figure, marking a significant stage in the rehabilitation of Shylock's dramatic possibilities.

Shylock's significance in the play consists largely of a certain relationship between ethnicity and economics; between racial and religious difference, and financial behaviour. The necessity for a historical perspective on the play is nowhere more apparent than in this matter of economics. A clear distinction is drawn in *The Merchant of Venice* between the respective commercial activities of Shylock and Antonio; and underlying that distinction is a clear moral separation, in Elizabethan thought, between different kinds of business dealing which in our modern capitalist economy would be very difficult to separate. This apparently absolute moral distinction rests on a sharp contrast between the two characters, which in a paradoxical way draws them together into a certain relationship of affinity. Although Antonio clearly belongs to the Christian community, he and Shylock tend to face each other as individuals with a common identity. There is even an analogy in the matter of race: since while most of the Venetian Christians display anti-semitism of a cultural kind, consisting mainly of racist humour and routine contempt, Antonio's racial hostility is much more active and concrete. It takes the form of a deliberate and determined commercial rivalry, based on a principled objection to the practice of *usury*.

It is commonly assumed by readers of the play that Shylock's fault is to charge 'excessive' interest on loans. This misapprehension rests on an understandable misreading of the word 'excess', which actually means, simply, 'interest'. Shylock lends money at interest and on security of property, land or person.

Antonio does not object to Shylock because he charges too much interest: he objects to the very idea that interest can be charged on loans at all. The distinction involved here is blurred for us because in the ethics governing the kind of modern economy to which we are accustomed, there is no such moral distinction between 'usury' and speculation, between what would now be called finance and venture capital. To think ourselves into this moral climate we would have to imagine a society in which financiers, and bank and building society managers, were hated and reviled, while company shareholders and speculators were regarded as irreproachably beneficial members of society.

In *The Merchant of Venice* however there is a fundamental, structural, ethical distinction between what Shylock and Antonio respectively do for a living. Antonio *trades*; he buys luxury goods from the East and West Indies, such as silks and spices, and sells them on the market in Venice. Antonio's speculative ventures involve *risk* (as the plot ultimately demonstrates), while Shylock's do not, since the usurer is bound to get either his money plus interest, or whatever security (such as the debtor's property and goods) has been bound over to him. The defaulting debtor became a criminal: so the law (in the case of Elizabethan England, a statute of 1571 making usury legal and open) could be seen as protecting the money-lender, where the speculative merchant would be risking everything in hazardous ventures which might at any moment turn to disaster.

These moral objections against usury were medieval in origin. A properly functioning feudal economy (in which land is exchanged for labour, and goods produced for use) has no place for money at all, let alone money-lending. The existence of money-lending on a large scale is a sure economic indicator that the feudal economy is breaking down, and giving way to capitalistic financial dealing. Medieval theology condemned usury as a sin, while the religious writers of the Protestant reformation, Luther and Calvin, accepted it as a necessity. Antonio in *The Merchant of Venice* is then, although a leading member of a new social class, the speculative entrepreneurial trader, has commercial ethics identical to those of an old class, the landowning aristocracy.

The play asks its audience to consider the difference between usury and speculative commerce not only in economic terms, but in the light of moral values. The business of the merchant is identified with friendship; that of the usurer with enmity. The former is regarded as disinterested and selfless; the other grasping and selfish, Antonio's trade is seen as an activity which enriches not only himself, but the life of the community as a whole. The exchange of money for goods is seen as fertilising, enriching, fruitful; while the exchange of money for money is assumed to be sterile, wasteful, profitless.

As I indicated earlier, Antonio doesn't confine himself to sermons and exhortations against usury, or even to voiding his phlegm on Jewish beards: he conducts an active, practical campaign against the usury he despises. Shylock hates him, because he is a Christian, 'But more, for that in low simplicity/ He lends out money gratis and brings down/ The rate of usance here with us in Venice' (I.3.40−42). Antonio goes further than this practice of cutting out the money-lenders by means of interest-free loans; he deliberately rescues defaulting debtors from the usurer's contract. Antonio admits that Shylock has come to hate him not from motiveless malignity, but because of this real and systematically inflicted commercial injury.

Both Shylock and Antonio are isolated from the remainder of the cast. Although the play, as the title indicates, is all about commerce, trade, financial dealing and exchange, only two of the leading characters are in fact directly involved in trade. Portia is a wealthy heiress, a landed proprietor. Bassanio lives on credit and by speculation on the marriage market. Gratiano, Salanio and Salerio are not merchants but speculators, Renaissance yuppies who live a carefree and irresponsible life on riches of unexplained origin. Lorenzo is, like Bassanio, poor and without means: he lives by abducting a wealthy heiress and persuading her to rob her father. The remaining characters are all servants or rulers.

In this way Shylock and Antonio are differentiated from the other characters, and placed (in different but related ways) outside the play's central community. They represent two opposed business ethics and two opposed moralities within the world of Venetian commerce. They are business rivals and competitors, enemies in trade and financial dealing. And in some strange way, they are very much alike. In what does this affinity lie?

Antonio is clearly isolated from the community of Christians, of which Bassanio is a natural member. Like Shylock, Antonio does not like masques and feasting. While the rest of the world is carefree and irresponsible, his role is to play a sad part. His melancholy, his loneliness, his sense of difference and isolation, all link him to his mighty opposite, Shylock. Antonio is at his most impressive when, under the experience of persecution, his language rises to the biblical dignity of Shylock's own eloquence: 'I am a tainted wether of the flock/Meetest for death' (IV.1.114–115).

The play opens with Antonio's supposedly mysterious and inexplicable melancholy. The reason for this sadness is in fact perfectly obvious: he loves Bassanio ('only loves the world for him'); he is not a lover of women, indignantly rejecting suggestions that he may be in love with one; and he is pointedly left out of the otherwise universal celebrations of marriage at the play's conclusion. His melancholy, then, is a response to the frustration of an unrequited homosexual love for Bassanio. When in the opening scene all the other characters leave the two men alone together, Antonio offers himself to Bassanio in plain though equivocal language: 'My purse, my person, my extremest means/ Lie all unlocked to your occasions' (I.1.138–139). 'Purse' and 'person' are linked in a very suggestive metaphor, as Antonio offers the 'extremities' of both fortune and body to his friend. Antonio's generosity and self-sacrifice are the more enhanced in dignity and beauty when we realise they are based in a love that can never be requited or fulfilled. Bassanio is, after all, a healthy red-blooded heterosexual, who seems to display if anything a certain callousness and insensitivity to the emotions of his friend.

In his *Divina Commedia* Dante placed usurers and sodomites (homosexuals) in the same circle of hell. Usury seemed to the medieval mind an unnatural way of doing a natural thing: that is, it was considered natural to create wealth and to prosper, but unnatural to do so by lending money at interest. The view that it was unnatural to make money 'breed' money, as the usurer does, could be found in Aristotle's *Ethics*; and this was connected with a similar moral distinction between heterosexual and homosexual love. To create wealth by the exchange of commodities for money was considered 'natural', and aligned with heterosexual love: each process could produce a third thing ('profit' or 'children') different from either. But money, as Aristotle insisted, is a *barren* metal, which cannot breed by itself. We find this economic controversy expressed in the play, when Shylock refutes a stock argument against usury by claiming that money can in practice, like Jacob's sheep, breed like a living thing.

The conventional ideas of Shakespeare's age upon these matters were not necessarily those of Shakespeare himself, and certainly they are not necessarily those embodied in the dialogic form of the play. In the medieval ideology inherited by the Renaissance, it was a fundamental insistence that homosexual love, love between man and man, was inevitably barren and sterile. In *The Merchant of Venice*, by contrast, we see such love capable of making everything out of nothing.

In two important passages of reported action, closely juxtaposed within a single scene, these two characters are polarised into a dialectical relationship of identity and opposition:

> SOLANIO I never heard a passion so confused,
> So strange, outrageous, and so variable
> As the dog Jew did utter in the streets:
> 'My daughter! O my ducats! O my daughter!
> Fled with a Christian! O my Christian ducats!
> Justice! The law! My ducats and my daughter!
> . . .'

> (II.2.12–17)

> SALERIO I saw Bassanio and Antonio part;
> Bassanio told him he would make some speed
> Of his return; he answered, 'Do not so.
> Slubber not business for my sake, Bassanio,
> But stay the very riping of the time.
> . . .
> And even there, his eye being big with tears,
> Turning his face, he put his hand behind him,
> And with affection wondrous sensible
> He wrung Bassanio's hand, and so they parted

> (II.8.36–40, 46–49)

The loss, in each case, of wealth and of affection, is identical: yet here the merchant and the usurer are polarised into a diametrical opposition. Shylock cannot distinguish ('My ducats and my daughter!') between human and material loss. Antonio, having already given, in financial terms, enough to render him vulnerable to bankruptcy and execution, and having yielded up his love to the embraces of a woman, can yet find it possible to give more. Bassanio should not, his friend insists, rush the business in which he is engaged merely for Antonio's sake. As Antonio turns his back on Bassanio he decorously hides his unmanly grief: yet at the same time places himself in the characteristic posture of homosexual intercourse. There could be no clearer distinction between the man who puts money on the same level as love, and the man who is prepared to 'give and hazard all he hath' for the sake of a love that can never bring him compensation or restitution.

Yet in another dramatic juxtaposition, the two appear as counterparts rather than opposites:

> SHYLOCK I'll have my bond! Speak not against my bond!
>
> SOLANIO I am sure the Duke
> Will never grant this forfeiture to hold.
> ANTONIO The Duke cannot deny the course of law,
> For the commodity that strangers have
> With us in Venice, if it be denied,
> Will much impeach the justice of the state,
> Since that the trade and profit of the city
> Consisteth of all nations.
>
> (III.3.4, 24–31)

Shylock here stands for justice, the law, and requires his legally permitted compensation for Antonio's non-performance of their contract ('bond'). Antonio, despite the fact that it is his own life and property that are forfeit, is fully in agreement with Shylock as to the justice of the usurer's cause. Antonio may speak the Christian language of compassion and mercy (though he showed little of either to Shylock), while Shylock appeals to the simple poetic justice of the Mosaic law. But both are in complete agreement on the validity of that internationalist law of Venice which regards all races as equal:

> ANTONIO The Duke cannot deny the course of law,
> For the commodity that strangers have

With us in Venice, if it be denied,
Will much impeach the justice of the state,
Since that the trade and profit of the city
Consisteth of all nations.

(III.3.26–31)

Within the context of Venetian law the problem remains insoluble, except that is by the forfeiture of Antonio's life. Dramatically, the plot here reaches a stalemate. The power to resolve the problem, which seems quite unavailable within the ethical and legal codes governing Venetian life and commerce, comes from a world very different from that modern financial centre: a world which could best be described as a romanticised, fantasy version of the traditional aristocracy: Belmont. Where Venice is a new world of risk and uncertainty, enterprise and competition, Belmont is a stable, established world, where the emphasis of social behaviour falls on obedience to tradition. In Venice there is no strong sense of family: most people seem to have no parents; those who do (like Jessica and Launcelot Gobbo) desert or abuse them. In Belmont, Portia acknowledges (not without some resistance) the validity of her dead father's will. Venice and Belmont seem to share a common morality, in that the best man is he who is prepared to 'give and hazard all', whether on the adventure of an argosy or the choice of a casket. Where however in Venice risk is perilously real, as we observe in the fate of Antonio, in Belmont the immanent logic of fairy tale (the third choice) guarantees the hero success.

In the trial scene Portia attempts to solve the deadlock by appeal to a universal natural law: she elevates the problem from one of law and finance, where there is no rational appeal beyond the justice of contract, to one of universal religion (though in fact of course there is nothing universal about Christianity), where the dominant value is mercy and forgiveness. She offers Shylock the opportunity of incorporation into a harmonised political economy where the Jew would rationally forfeit his legal rights in the interests of the public good. Shylock's refusal — a resistance in which the determined fundamentalism of religious faith and the stubborn reality of economic forces are joined — renders this solution impossible. Having failed in her attempt at incorporation, Portia openly proceeds to use the power of Christian nationalism against him. Underlying the superficial multi-culturalism of that cosmopolitan Venetian law used by Shylock and respected by Antonio, lies a judicial structure designed to protect Venetian citizens against aliens. When the internationalist and egalitarian spirit of progressive capitalism produces a resistance challenging its hegemony, it is quite willing to use older judicial codes to defend the native against the foreigner. Shylock is finally proven right: he was never, in the last instance, considered by Venice as anything other than an outsider.

The 'mercy' ultimately offered to Shylock by the victorious Christian community — to keep his life without his property — is a fate described earlier by Antonio as one worse than death. Ultimately the play's careful consideration and comparison of these two kinds of 'otherness', racial and sexual, is decided primarily on economic grounds. The proposed alliance between the new speculative merchant class and the traditional aristocracy is strong enough both to suppress the dangerous power of finance capital in foreign hands, and to embrace the sexual difference of the solitary Antonio. The 'comic' resolution, seen from the perspective of history, hardly seems 'comic' at all.

AFTERTHOUGHTS

1

Explain the relevance to Holderness's argument of the comparison with *Twelfth Night* (pages 30–31).

2

What do you understand by 'dialectical' (pages 32 and 37)?

3

Are you persuaded by Holderness's argument that Antonio and Shylock are 'in some strange way . . . very much alike' (page 35)?

4

What differences does Holderness highlight in this essay between Venice and Belmont (page 39)? Do you agree with the view of Venice put forward at the close of the essay?

Mark Thornton Burnett

Mark Thornton Burnett taught at the University of Geneva before taking up his present post as lecturer in English at the Queen's University of Belfast. He has published extensively on Elizabethan and Jacobean drama.

ESSAY

'I know not why I am so sad': ideas of character in *The Merchant of Venice*

In an article published in 1916, Ernest Hunter Wright quotes from critics writing about Shakespeare in the eighteenth and nineteenth centuries who eulogised in highly romantic terms the transcendent powers of the artist's imagination:

> We may begin with the familiar miracle of the reality of Shakspere's characters . . . Shakspere 'is not so much an imitator,' in the consummate phrase of Pope, 'as an instrument of nature . . . Every single character in Shakspere is as much an individual as those of life itself.' And though with the last sentence Johnson may be in verbal disagreement, with the whole position he is in enthusiastic concord. 'Shakspere is . . . the poet that holds up to his readers a faithful mirror of manners and of life. His characters are the progeny of common humanity' . . . even the idolators of the romantic period [argued] . . . that the characters in these plays are as nearly living beings as any other characters to be found in books.

The article promises to offer an alternative way of interpreting

Shakespearean characters but, in fact, does nothing of the sort. For Wright goes on to approve the sentiments he ostensibly challenges and only slightly changes the direction of previous arguments. 'Shakspere's people are the purest copies that we have of real people', he writes, adding, the dramatist 'gives us characters that retain . . . the irregularity of actual men and women to present to us . . . the puzzle [that] life presents . . .'.[1] This is not very different from the subjective, flowery expressions of those scholars who approached Shakespeare centuries earlier.

I would like to attempt a fresh critical method. I will be asking how we can understand 'character' in Shakespeare, and will be suggesting that characters in *The Merchant of Venice* are not necessarily representations of 'real people'; instead, they are functions, constructions and embodiments of recurring themes. It is with these suggestions in mind, and with reference to the issues of identity, economy, exchange, mercantilism and race, that I intend to pursue my argument.

The conversation at the opening of the play might tempt us to try to find out what troubles Antonio, the merchant, one of the speakers:

> ANTONIO In sooth I know not why I am so sad.
> It wearies me, you say it wearies you;
> But how I caught it, found it, or came by it,
> What stuff 'tis made of, whereof it is born,
> I am to learn;
> And such a want-wit sadness makes of me
> That I have much ado to know myself.
> SALERIO Your mind is tossing on the ocean,
> There where your argosies with portly sail,
> Like signors and rich burghers on the flood,
> Or as it were the pageants of the sea,
> Do overpeer the petty traffickers
> That curtsy to them, do them reverence,
> As they fly by them with their woven wings.

(I.1.1–14)

---

[1] 'Reality and Inconsistency in Shakspere's Characters', in Brander Matthews and Ashley Horace Thorndike (eds), *Shaksperian Studies* (New York, 1916), pp. 371–372, 382, 401.

It seems useful here to suggest that Antonio is a type struggling to define and place himself, grappling with an unknowable malaise. His questions about origins, about suffering, about forms of persecution and about identity, all have a bearing on the preoccupations the play goes on to examine. What Salerio says is similarly important. In an extended simile, he sees human activity as in thrall to the larger flux of the maritime market. The signors and burghers overshadow the petty traffickers (Shylock might be numbered in the latter category) while the gesture of female humility (the curtsy) suggests the existence of a society in which women are subordinated. (Against this society, of course, Portia and Jessica will endeavour to achieve fulfilment.) Finally, the reference to the pageant implies insubstantiality; already, *The Merchant of Venice*, through the characters, is introducing the major themes and sounding warning notes about the fragile underside of economic prosperity.

The opening of the following scene develops these ideas, playing a variation on the theme of the shaping of character by economic forces. Portia, like Antonio, presents herself as a person to be scrutinised and interpreted: 'By my troth, Nerissa, my little body is aweary of this great world' (I.2.1–2). The way in which she describes herself points to the oppression under which she labours. Bound to select a husband according to the dictates of her father's will, Portia is weighed down by the injunctions of a ghostly parent. Money, in the form of Portia's inheritance, now becomes a source both of power and of anxiety.

Identity and economy emerge as some of the play's dominant concerns. This claim can be reinforced when we consider Launcelot Gobbo, Shylock's servant, another character tied to an economic arrangement. A dialogue with his father runs:

> GOBBO   I cannot think you are my son.
> LAUNCELOT   I know not what I shall think of that; but I am Launcelot, the Jew's man, and I am sure Margery your wife is my mother.
>
> (II.2.80–83)

In this witty conversation, Gobbo is impelled, like the other characters, to pin himself down and to define himself. The exchange also has an unsettling effect for a parent does not know his child and doubts are raised about marital fidelity.

A connection can be made between identity and economy and the associated themes of contract, exchange and prejudice. It is worth reiterating that the problem of finding a social place is exacerbated by the onerous contractual agreements which determine the conduct of the majority of the characters and keep Venice and Belmont in a state of virtual imprisonment. Bassanio is in debt to Antonio who, in turn, is bound to Shylock (the pound of flesh). Jessica strives to release herself from the powerful hold of her tyrannical father. Launcelot Gobbo, at his first appearance, grapples with two voices contending for the possession of his soul.

> Certainly my conscience will serve me to run from this Jew my master. The fiend is at mine elbow and tempts me, saying to me, 'Gobbo, Launcelot Gobbo, good Launcelot,' or 'Good Gobbo,' or 'Good Launcelot Gobbo, use your legs, take the start, run away.' My conscience says, 'No, take head, honest Launcelot, take heed, honest Gobbo,' or as aforesaid, 'Honest Launcelot Gobbo, do not run, scorn running with thy heels.'
>
> (II.2.1–8)

But the emphasis of the scene lies less with Gobbo than with the structure of compacts to which he belongs: the servant is not alone in trying to come to terms with constraining ties. His view thus colours our perception of the debates presented elsewhere, accentuating and distancing them at one and the same time. The servant's conversation with himself performs other tasks, too: Jessica's embracing of Christianity is prefigured in Gobbo's dropping one master and joining another. His finding another place for himself also prepares the way for the passing at the end of Shylock's wealth to the Christian community.

The passage in which Shylock considers Antonio's status as a merchant illuminates the larger, mercantilist contractual system in which all of the characters are implicated.

> Ho no, no, no, no! My meaning in saying he is a good man is to have you understand me that he is sufficient. Yet his means are in supposition. He hath an argosy bound to Tripolis, another to the Indies; I understand, moreover, upon the Rialto, he hath a third at Mexico, a fourth for England, and other ventures he hath squandered abroad. But ships are but boards, sailors but

men; there be land rats and water rats, water thieves and land
thieves, I mean pirates; and then there is the peril of waters,
winds, and rocks. The man is, not withstanding, sufficient.
Three thousand ducats; I think I may take his bond.

(I.3.15–26)

Part of the interest of the speech is that it presents individuals
as being controlled by an economic process. Antonio is in the
grip of a system where all things are reduced (ships, for example,
are like 'boards'). Exploitation is reciprocal: merchants are
thieves who are themselves preyed upon by pirates. The passage
is of particular relevance as far as Shylock is concerned for he is
at once the victim of Venice but also its exponent: the society he
lives in both sustains and destroys his enterprises.

One other structure confines independent action in the play,
and it is erected upon the soil of racial expectations. Portia is
pursued by suitors who come from a variety of countries; one of
them is the Prince of Morocco, and he woos in exaggerated
terms:

Mislike me not for my complexion,
The shadowed livery of the burnished sun,
To whom I am a neighbour and near bred.
Bring me the fairest creature northward born,
Where Phoebus' fire scarce thaws the icicles,
And let us make incision for your love
To prove whose blood is reddest, his or mine.
I tell thee, lady, this aspect of mine
Hath feared the valiant. By my love I swear,
The best-regarded virgins of our clime
Have loved it too. I would not change this hue,
Except to steal your thoughts, my gentle queen.

(II.1.1–12)

An African type in this scene strives to overcome the barriers of
prejudice by playing upon the prejudice. He alludes to assumptions about his conduct to counter possible objections to his
courtship and to elevate himself. However, his words are more
complicated than this assessment might suggest, and there are
also contradictions. Violent opposites are brought together (heat
is set against cold, and white is contrasted to red and black), and

veiled threats about violation and theft emerge (the word, 'incision', carries sexual meanings). The Prince is dramatised both as a refined courtier and as a lascivious stereotype.

In this way, the persuasions of Portia's suitors indicate that characters in *The Merchant of Venice* make efforts to resist social forces that are oppressive and exploitative. What other attempts do the characters make? One way of reading characters in the play is to imagine them as examples of energies that question the behaviour of the privileged. Much of the play, for instance, focuses upon the position of women in a stratified society. Portia and Jessica are both, at the start, caught up in a network of tangled obligations. In addition, Portia is regarded by the male characters as a source of wealth and a sexual object. Bassanio states:

> In Belmont is a lady richly left,
> And she is fair, and, fairer than that word,
> Of wondrous virtues. Sometimes from her eyes
> I did receive fair speechless messages.
> Her name is Portia, nothing undervalued
> To Cato's daughter, Brutus' Portia;
> Nor is the wide world ignorant of her worth,
> For the four winds blow in from every coast
> Renowned suitors, and her sunny locks
> Hang on her temples like a golden fleece,
> Which makes her seat of Belmont Colchos' strond,
> And many Jasons come in quest of her.
> O my Antonio, had I but the means
> To hold a rival place with one of them,
> I have a mind presages me such thrift
> That I should questionless be fortunate.

(I.1.161–176)

Bassanio's description of Portia uses mythological references and financial puns, and one observes that she is first drawn in the language of trade and economy that is, in the play, particularly distinctive. It is as if Portia, in being sought by aspirants from all corners of the world, becomes just another piece of merchandise.

Certainly women in *The Merchant of Venice* do take on unconventional abilities. Jessica dresses as a boy, and her disguise permits her a greater freedom and movement. Throwing down to Lorenzo, her lover, Shylock's money, she suggests that the change in her sex allows her to behave with a new flexibility and courage:

> Here, catch this casket; it is worth the pains.
> I am glad 'tis night, you do not look on me,
> For I am much ashamed of my exchange.
> But love is blind, and lovers cannot see
> The pretty follies that themselves commit;
> For if they could, Cupid himself would blush
> To see me thus transformèd to a boy.
>
> (II.6.33–39)

Economic terminology mingles with expressions of conventional female modesty in Jessica's rushed injunctions. At the same time, as she celebrates the powers to which she is now entitled, she anticipates difficulties in her relationship with Lorenzo arising from the assumption of unfamiliar privileges.

One approach to character in *The Merchant of Venice* is, then, to attend to the play's investigation of attempts to establish a stable identity in the face of hostile economic forces, contracts and a prejudiced way of thinking that favours the elite. This is to argue for a dark *The Merchant of Venice* and not for the comedy that is insisted upon by some critics. In this respect, it would be appropriate to discuss issues of comedy and tragedy and to consider how they feature in the play's structural movement. The Belmont scenes have often been analysed as lightening tensions after the troubling conflicts of the Venetian sections of the play. It is also possible to suggest that they do not seem to present an alternative society as they occupy themselves with the issues of the main plot but address them from a different perspective. Bassanio's ruminations before the caskets are a case in point; he exclaims:

> The world is still deceived with ornament.
> In law, what plea so tainted and corrupt,
> But being seasoned with a gracious voice,
> Obscures the show of evil? In religion,
> What damnèd error but some sober brow
> Will bless it and approve it with a text,

Hiding the grossness with fair ornament?
. . .
        Look on beauty,
And you shall see 'tis purchased by the weight,
Which therein works a miracle in nature,
Making them lightest that wear most of it.

(III.2.74–80, 88–91)

Deceit is the main idea that preoccupies Bassanio, and this is
not surprising as his choice of the right casket is the factor upon
which winning Portia depends (Portia can also be said to cheat
in that the song contains clues that will enable Bassanio to
make the correct decision). But his speech has a chill resonance
when placed in the context of the play as a whole. His reference
to corruption in the legal system casts a glance ahead to Portia's
role in the trial of Shylock and prevents an easy identification
with his sentiments. The hypocrisy in religion, to which Bassanio
alludes, also brings to mind how Christians in the play use
religion to justify their own unjust practices. And, of course, the
detail of weighing beauty is a reminder of Antonio; Bassanio's
lofty rhetoric has been enabled by happily exploiting, once more,
his friend's financial generosity. Belmont and Venice, ultimately,
do not seem to be very far apart.

Portia, of Belmont, enters Venetian society when she dresses
as a lawyer to come to Antonio's defence at the trial. Her
persuasions achieve a grandeur of utterance and a delicacy of
poetic pronouncement:

The quality of mercy is not strained,
It droppeth as the gentle rain from heaven
Upon the place beneath. It is twice blest,
It blesseth him that gives and him that takes.
'Tis mightiest in the mightiest, it becomes
The thronèd monarch better than his crown.

(IV.1.181–186)

Her speech does have mercy, liberty and justice as its themes,
but it is not matched by similar acts of mercy in the Christian
community. Portia does not practise what she preaches, and her
appeals to divine authority, because of what has taken place
earlier, make us suspicious. Her plea is incongruous when

considered in relation to the surrounding scenes. That she allows the Duke to deliver the final judgement, moreover, and retires from the action after having taken such an active part, somewhat invalidates her noble aspirations.

Comedy does feature towards the end (as in the lovers' dispute between Jessica and Lorenzo), but the closing stages are simultaneously tonally shifting and inconsistent. In the final scene, Portia reveals the truth about the trial to Antonio, and Nerissa tells Gratiano of the charade:

> NERISSA   And pardon me, my gentle Gratiano,
> For that same scrubbèd boy, the doctor's clerk,
> In lieu of this last night did lie with me.
> GRATIANO   Why, this is like the mending of highways
> In summer, where the ways are fair enough.
> What, are we cuckolds ere we have deserved it?
>
> (V.1.260–265)

A number of ideas are operating in her confessional provocation. In saying that she lay with the doctor's clerk, she is offering a statement of independence and a refusal to be tied to the wifely obligations that she will soon have to embrace. Gratiano's response is also barbed in that he entertains the possibility of marital conflict, and this casts a shadow over the comic surface of the final scenes.

Gratiano, indeed, has the final lines:

> PORTIA   It is almost morning,
> And yet I am sure you are not satisfied
> Of these events at full. Let us go in,
> And charge us there upon inter'gatories,
> And we will answer all things faithfully.
> GRATIANO   Let it be so. The first inter'gatory
> That my Nerissa shall be sworn on is
> Whether till the next night she had rather stay,
> Or go to bed now, being two hours to day.
> But were the day come, I should wish it dark
> Till I were couching with the doctor's clerk.
> Well, while I live I'll fear no other thing
> So sore as keeping safe Nerissa's ring.
>
> (V.1.295–307)

The concluding dialogue shows each character voicing doubts about the extent of the other's commitment. Portia, first, suggests that Gratiano and her husband will not be satisfied because men, by nature, and distrustful. She proposes a mock-trial in which all will be revealed, but the plan is uncomfortably close to the other trial that has already taken place in which justice was perverted, while the use of the word 'faithfully' strikes a discordant note as fidelity, in the play as a whole, has been singularly absent. Gratiano's speech is disjunctive, but in another sense. There is a confusion (if not conflation) of female and male, and an uncertainty over the person with whom he intends to consummate the marriage; the reminder that Nerissa dressed as a boy recalls the intimacy of Antonio and Bassanio and the former's exclusion from the celebrations. Sexual lines of demarcation do not seem to have been realigned. The play ends, too, with a bawdy joke. The 'ring' ostensibly refers to the 'ring' Gratiano wore and which he was persuaded to yield to the doctor's clerk. But it also signifies Nerissa's sexual parts and, in this light, the word 'sore' reflects unpleasantly upon Gratiano's lustful intentions. He himself closes by expressing an anxiety about Nerissa's future chastity which jars with the comic impetus of the play in its unsuccessful attempts to restore harmony and order.

I have tried to suggest in this essay that we should endeavour to prevent ourselves from identifying with Shakespearean characters as 'real people' but, rather, to comprehend them as voicers of attitudes, as undermining energies or as the products of social and economic forces. In *The Merchant of Venice*, the characters are part of the play's exploration of the instabilities of identity in a specific economic situation which is contested from many quarters. The play does not resolve the issues it raises, but this does not mean that we should pass upon it an unfavourable judgement. *The Merchant of Venice* highlights a range of questions, and it is part of its complexity that we continue to look for answers.

AFTERTHOUGHTS

1

Explain the importance to Thornton Burnett's argument of the passage quoted at the beginning of this essay (page 42).

2

What parallels does Thornton Burnett suggest between the first Launcelot Gobbo scene (II.2) and the play's major themes (pages 44–45)?

3

Do you agree that Portia is viewed by the male characters of the play as a 'piece of merchandise' (page 47)?

4

Do you agree with Thornton Burnett's interpretation of the final Act of the play (pages 50–51)?

Peter Thomson

Peter Thomson is Professor of Drama at Exeter University, and the author of numerous critical works.

ESSAY

Stolen by Shylock: a stage theft

A reading of *The Merchant of Venice* is prefaced with a puzzle. How has it come about that a character who appears in only five of the play's twenty scenes, and who is altogether absent from the final Act, has so dominated the audience's responses? It is a domination that has lasted at least since 1741, when Charles Macklin first played the part. As John Russell Brown astutely points out:

> [Shylock] often takes the final curtain-call, without Portia or Bassanio, without Antonio, the merchant of Venice. This tradition is so strong that it is easy to forget how strange it is: how odd that a villain — the one who threatens the happiness of the others — should so run away with a play that is a comedy by other signs, and that makes only a passing unconcerned allusion to him at its conclusion. But the records are unequivocal. In the theatre it is his play.[1]

---

[1] J R Brown, *Shakespeare's Plays in Performance*, (London, 1966), p. 71.

I shall go on to argue that this may not always have been true and that Shakespeare neither intended nor expected it to happen. But I should, first, pay attention to some of the other crucial questions that demand answers from the director and designer in what has become, in the modern theatre, the crucial pre-rehearsal period. They must ask, not only 'what kind of Shylock will this one be?', but also:

1 In what kind of Venice are this merchant and this usurer to be placed?

2 How can the contrasting qualities of Portia be best reinforced by the scenic (or atmospheric) distinctness of Belmont? The contrast is, of course, already embedded in Shakespeare's language, of which the name Belmont (meaning, literally, 'beautiful mountain') is only the label. But the theatre must still work to realise it. Is this home of Portia's to be a Fiesole, smiling down on Florence; a castle in the shaded hills above old Stratford to the north; a beautiful feminine mountain (a *'mons Veneris'*) towering over the flat, masculine seascape of the commercially competitive rat-race-city of Venice?

3 How can attractive life be breathed into Bassanio, who, without it, is not much more than a gold-digging, bisexual stud? Unlike Romeo among the revellers of Verona, Bassanio is only with difficulty made distinct by love from the other Flash Harries of the Rialto.

4 How much of the audience's emotional guidance can be safely entrusted to the difficult-to-play Launcelot Gobbo?

5 And is Act V inevitably an anticlimax after the ferociously brilliant trial scene and Shylock's last exit? By 1879, when Henry Irving staged his great production at the Lyceum, Act V was customarily omitted, all its essential action having been relocated in Act IV; and Irving's (admittedly half-hearted) attempt to restore it was vetoed by the Lyceum faithful. For them, nothing was left of the play once Henry's Shylock had gone.

On the answers to such production questions as these, more than the role of Shylock depends, but that is not to say that the role of Shylock does not depend on them. Performers, we must always recognise, need to interrogate the text of a play with a visual intensity that is not required of a reader. The impact of a 'new'

Shylock will be conditioned by the answer to a simple-sounding question: 'What shall this Shylock look like?' Critics may duck the issue of the cut of the Jewish gaberdine, the one that Antonio evidently has the unhygienic habit of spitting on (I.3.109), but the theatre cannot. And the alarming, or at the very least challenging, fact is that much of the play's emotional impact in a particular theatre at a particular time will depend upon decisions taken by a costume-designer.

When, as a boy, I saw Emlyn Williams play Shylock at Stratford, my child's imagination could scarcely distinguish him from Fagin. Look at the photographs of Herbert Beerbohm Tree. Where did his Svengali end and his Shylock begin? In California in 1985, I saw a Shylock modelled on Disraeli: dapper, dandified and deceitful. Olivier, in Jonathan Miller's production (preserved on television) was more of a Rothschild, urbane and confident along the corridors of power. Why, after all, should Shylock live in a ghetto? Why not in a house like the one Leopold Rothschild owned at 5 Hamilton Place, now perhaps the plushest private club in London? What Shylock wears determines from the start what Shylock is, but the role-model is not, in the twentieth century, single or simple. The range from Fagin through Svengali and Disraeli to Rothschild is wide, and can always be extended. Why not a black Shylock,[2] or an Iraqi Shylock, or an Aristotle Onassis in Venice? Some models, we might reasonably argue, are more legitimate than others. But there is no getting away from the fact that, in the theatre at least, the general response to *The Merchant of Venice* will be conditioned by the decision on how to dress Shylock.

There are, I suggest, few clearer examples of the way in which history can modify or even transform a text. When Shakespeare wrote *The Merchant of Venice*, there was precious little cause for anti-semitism, whether religious or commercial, in England. There may have been as few as one hundred Jews in the whole country, certainly not enough to threaten the livelihood of Christian merchants in the capital. As for religious controversy, the continuing Catholic threat and the emergence

---

[1] Shylock was, in fact, a favoured part in the repertoire of the first great black American actor, Ira Aldridge (1807–67).

of radical Protestantism as a political force were more likely to engage contemporary passions than the question of whether the New Testament could properly share a book-binding with the Old Testament. There was, of course, the famous case of Elizabeth I's Jewish physician, Dr Lopez, whose execution in 1594 for supposedly plotting the death of the Queen has entered into scholarly debate on the precise dating of the play; but one Jew no more makes a pogrom than one swallow makes a summer. Shakespeare had no genealogy of stage Jews from which to construct Shylock's genealogy.[3] Shylock's comic ancestry can be traced back to Roman comedy: a conventional old miser, conventionally outwitted by young lovers. This is a character who would soon appear fully drawn in Molière's *L'Avare* as Harpagon. More pertinently, he is the antagonist of many of the *commedia dell'arte* scenarios contemporaneously maturing in Italy. Shylock — the 'original' Shylock — is, in part, Pantalone, one of the *zanni* of a commedia scenario, whose initial repressiveness is a provocation to young love.[4] The overthrow of Pantalone is, in effect, an assertion of the joyfulness in youth and of the rights due to love. Shylock is a Pantalone gulled of his daughter and his ducats. This is certainly how Thomas Doggett played him in the first post-Restoration revival of the play in 1701. Doggett in silhouette (long nose, jutting beard) is Pantalone, and his costume is Pantalone's, too. But the passage of time was already eroding the Shakespearean rock of the text. The 1701 performance was a typical example of Shakespeare 'improved' to suit the more refined taste of the time, 'improved' in this instance by Lord Lansdowne, who chose as his title, not the *Merchant*, but *The Jew of Venice*. Even so, and despite the significant change of title, the play presented to the London audience at the opening of the eighteenth century was emphatically a comedy of the kind that the splendidly irascible William Poel hoped to revive two centuries later:

---

[3] The isolated example of Marlowe's eccentric *The Jew of Malta* (c. 1589) is insufficient to constitute a genealogy.

[4] A typical scenario in the improvised performances of a *commedia dell'arte* troupe would invite the audience to delight in the triumph of youthful lovers over the aged Pantalone's attempts to keep them apart. It was a function of the *zanni*, of whom Pantalone is one, to be fooled.

The basis of Shakespeare's comedy is a romantic story of love and adventure. It shows us a lovable and high-minded heroine, her adventurous and fervent lover, and his unselfish friend, together with their merry companions and sweethearts. And into this happy throng, for the purpose of having a villain, the dramatist thrusts the morose and malicious usurer, who is intended to be laughed at and defeated, not primarily because he is a Jew, but because he is a curmudgeon; thus the prodigal defeats the miser.[5]

It was always Poel's intention, against the tide of nineteenth-century fashions of elaborate pictorial staging, to present Shakespeare's plays as they might have been originally presented at the Elizabethan playhouses. The comedy he describes is the comedy he believes Shakespeare wrote; and we have to concede that he may be right (though always with the proviso that, if Shakespeare wanted his Shylock to be *merely* a villain, he made the mistake of endowing him with language and passions that split the seams of villainy). But the passage of time, as I have said, modifies a text, and the changes, though scarcely discernible in general, have sometimes the force of sudden revelations.

So it was that *The Merchant of Venice* was transformed on St Valentine's Day in 1741, when the extraordinary Irish actor Charles Macklin first performed what the poet Alexander Pope called 'the Jew/ That Shakespeare drew'. It was, we should be clear, no part of Macklin's intention to soften a cruel portrait. His aim was to harden a comic–grotesque one. I doubt whether Macklin's Shylock had any of the tragic dimensions that seem appropriate now to such set pieces as:

> I am a Jew. Hath not a Jew eyes? Hath not a Jew hands, organs, dimensions, senses, affections, passions? Fed with the same food, hurt with the same weapons, subject to the same diseases, healed by the same means, warmed and cooled by the same winter and summer as a Christian is? If you prick us, do we not bleed? If you tickle us, do we not laugh?
>
> (III.1.53–59)

---

[5] William Poel, *Shakespeare in the Theatre* (London, 1913), p. 77.

Between Macklin's performance and the present day, after all, a holocaust has intervened. Can anyone seriously argue that *The Merchant of Venice* remains the same play if performed in the Lebanon in 1990 as it would have been in Auschwitz in 1944? Books may occupy space, but the dimension of theatre is time. By 1741, there was, in London, a Jewish ghetto of about 20,000 to provide a context within which Macklin began the new history of Shylock; a history that has, over the subsequent 250 years, given us a range of Jewish usurers from the monumentally implacable gangster to the martyred victim of Christian bigotry. In order to thrive in eighteenth-century England, the Jewish community had to be commercially shrewd. None of the professions was open to them. The legal profession became the first, but not until 1820, and no Jew was admitted to a municipal post until 1843. That is to say that, in 1741 far more than in 1594, there was a genuine 'Jewish question', and the text of *The Merchant of Venice* was transformed by it.

So what happened to Shylock? Before the end of the eighteenth century, the London theatre had made a measurable contribution to the softening of attitudes towards Jews, if not through Shylock, then through a conscious counter-Shylock. The play in question was Richard Cumberland's *The Jew*, first performed in 1794. Cumberland's title role belongs, not to Shylock, but to Sheva, who has this to say of himself early in the play:

> The world knows no great deal of me. I do not deny but my monies may roll a little, but for myself I do not roll at all. I live sparingly and labour hard, therefore I am called a miser — I cannot help it — an uncharitable dog — I must endure it — a bloodsucker, an extortioner, a Shylock — hard names, Mr Frederic; but what can a poor Jew say in return, if a Christian chooses to abuse him?

On the face of it, then, Sheva is quite like Shylock. He even has a Gobbo-like comic servant whom he starves. But Sheva has a secret. He is 'good', as even the starving servant acknowledges. He saves money, spends nothing on himself, in order to give it away to deserving people: 'I love my monies, I do love them dearly; but I love my fellow-creatures a little better.' It is Sheva's generosity that paves the way for the play's happy ending, and the whole purpose behind the persistent Shakespearean allusions in this popular play is to provide a counter-play to *The Merchant of Venice.*

Cumberland's play would have had no point if Shylock's domination of Shakespeare's text were not already well established. It was a part that attracted all the great tragic actors of the nineteenth century. Edmund Kean made his sensational debut in it in 1814. His Shylock was awesome, 'like a chapter of Genesis' to the eyes of the young Douglas Jerrold. George Frederick Cooke's was a depraved demon, Charles Kean's as unsentimentalised as his father's. It was Irving's 1879 performance that opened the door to sentiment, and the key to the door was a father's love for his daughter, Shylock's love for Jessica. The American actor Richard Mansfield, who derived many of his best effects from Irving, always greeted his Jessica (II.5.9) with a tender kiss. On such single stage gestures, whole interpretations turn. The love of fathers for daughters was no less idealised in Victorian fiction than the love of mothers for sons. The actress Helen Faucit, who had played Portia to Macready's Shylock before abandoning the stage to marry an art-loving banker, published her vaporous reflections on the after-life of the play in her retirement:

> I think that the Jew will not live long. His body and mind have been too sorely bruised and shaken. But Portia's spell will be upon him to the end. His last looks will be upon the eyes which have opened his, and shown him the 'light to lighten his darkness'; and he who was despised, reviled, and himself at war with all men, will now have felt the happiness of bestowing forgiveness, and the blessed hope of being himself forgiven.[6]

But this same Helen Faucit, so gentle to Shylock, is full of criticism for Jessica:

> As her character improves, becoming chastened and ennobled, she will reflect upon the graceless step she took in leaving her old, lonely father, whatever might have been his faults, and in robbing him, too. How can she look for happiness in her wedded

---

[6] Helen Faucit, *Some of Shakespeare's Female Characters* (London, 1899), p. 42. The subsequent quotation is from the same page.

life, she who has commenced it so unworthily? Oh that she could make reparation! She must know the sentence passed upon her father in the court at Venice. How, then, can she be happy? And so some day, permission being obtained by Portia, she may be seen at the feet of the old man, there sobbing out her grief and her contrition; and he will remember that he made her 'home a hell', and look gently upon her.

Helen Faucit, like so many Victorians, was over-stuffed with a diet of inferior Tennyson, but her sentimental meditations are representative of post-Irving responses to *The Merchant of Venice*. For generations of theatregoers, the tragedy of Shylock has cast a blight over the comedy of Portia and Bassanio; and Faucit's distorting mirror does serve to reflect a moment in the play which is crucial for the actor of Shylock. It is in Act II scene 5, and only there, that we see him with his daughter. Much will depend on what he makes of it. Irving, who left nothing to chance, interpolated a silent scene after Act II scene 6. The Lyceum audience saw Jessica and Lorenzo slide offstage in a gondola, and there followed a sort of street carnival with lights and revelry until the curtain fell. And while the audience applauded, the curtain rose again on an empty stage, dimly lit. Then, in the distance but growing closer, was heard the tapping of a stick — the sound of Shylock returning home to his daughter. He crosses the bridge over the canal that has carried Jessica away for ever, he stands at the door of his house, eventually he knocks, knocks again. There is no answer. Ellen Terry, who played Portia in the production, recalled this moment much later: 'For absolute pathos, achieved by absolute simplicity of means, I never saw anything in the theatre to compare with it'.[7] I believe her.

There is no doubt at all that Irving's Shylock purloined the play, as, more recently (1988) and to a very different end, did Antony Sher's. But who did he purloin it from? The answer, probably, is Antonio. But, if so, was the fault Irving's or Shakespeare's? The actor of Antonio is provided with poor material for a title role. Has a weaker first entrance ever been

---

[7] Ellen Terry, *The Story of My Life* (London, 1908), p. 186.

devised? This is how the play opens:

> *Enter Antonio, Salerio, and Solanio.*
> ANTONIO   In sooth I know not why I am so sad.
> It wearies me, you say it wearies you

Here he comes, the 'hero', and what does he say? 'I don't know why I'm so miserable. I bore myself, and I evidently bore everybody else'. And five Acts later, after spending most of the intervening time moping, he is the only partnerless person at the final curtain, when Portia and Bassanio, Gratiano and Nerissa, and Lorenzo and Jessica run headlong from the stage to make merry and to make babies. There is certainly something sad about Antonio's aloneness at the end of the play, but sadness never reaches higher than the knees of tragedy. It is very difficult indeed for an actor to make much of Antonio. In the theatre, I have always been relieved when the first scene, with its stilted Venetian verse, is over and we can move to the unexpected prose of Belmont. Act I scene 2 is, I suppose, an indoor scene. With the single exception of the trial in Act IV, all of Venice is street-scenes (the greatest number in Shakespeare). Where else can Jew and Gentile meet? To get indoors, we have to go to Belmont. This is a contrast that serves to reinforce all the other differences between Venice and Belmont; but there is, to begin with, a striking similarity. Like Antonio, Portia enters in mid-conversation confessing to world-weariness: 'By my troth, Nerissa, my little body is aweary of this great world.' We can presume that the unstated cause of sadness in Antonio and Portia is the same — Bassanio. The story of the first three Acts is a variant of the familiar love-triangle, with Portia and Antonio at each end of the base line and Bassanio, unconvincingly, at the apex. The frequent transitions from Venice to Belmont posed unanswerable problems for the nineteenth-century stage, where each new setting had to be fully built and pictorially impressive. As a result, the Belmont scenes were constantly cut, transposed or merged. Such radical rearrangement violates the structural precision of the play. Shakespeare's strategy, perhaps his major achievement, in *The Merchant of Venice* is to create suspense through the employment of 'imminence'. What is about to happen in Venice or in Belmont is constantly interrupted by a shift to the other place. The effect can be perceived through a simple listing of the location and approximate stage-time of the scenes for a performance that lasts about 150 minutes.

I.1   *Venice* (10 minutes). Our appetites are whetted by mention of Portia and Belmont.

I.2   *Belmont* (10 minutes). The scene ends with the Prince of Morocco's arrival *imminent*.

I.3   *Venice* (10 minutes). The scene ends with the signing of the bond *imminent*.

II.1   *Belmont* (5 minutes). The scene ends with Morocco's choice of casket *imminent*.

II.2—II.6   *Venice* (20 minutes). This sequence of scenes is unusual in Shakespeare. It amounts to being a 'meanwhile, back in Venice' sequence. The very same 20 minutes are passing in Belmont. At the end of the sequence, Bassanio's departure for Belmont is *imminent*.

II.7   *Belmont* (5 minutes). Twenty minutes later than II.1, Morocco makes his fatal choice.

II.8   *Venice* (3 minutes). The scene ends with Antonio's learning of a foundered ship *imminent*.

II.9   *Belmont* (6 minutes). The Prince of Arragon makes his fatal choice, but the scene ends with the arrival of Bassanio *imminent*.

III.1   *Venice* (5 minutes). The scene ends with Antonio's ruin *imminent*.

III.2   *Belmont* (15 minutes). A crucial scene in the comic plot. Bassanio makes his choice of casket. With marriage imminent, this could be the last scene of a comedy, but it ends with Bassanio's departure (to avert Antonio's tragedy) *imminent*.

III.3   *Venice* (2 minutes). A short, sharp shock of a scene, which ends with Antonio's death *imminent*.

III.4   *Belmont* (4 minutes). The scene ends with Portia's surprise departure for Venice *imminent*.

III.5   *Belmont* (4 minutes). On the Elizabethan stage, this would not have been separated from the previous scene, but Shakespeare did not find it easy to assimilate Lorenzo and Jessica into his rapid story-telling structure.

IV.1   *Venice* (30 minutes). The trial scene brings the Venetian part of the plot to its climax. Only when the knife is sharpened and ready to plunge into Antonio's bared breast does Portia, grandmistress of imminence, intervene.

IV.2   *Venice* (1 minute). With Bassanio already discomforted by the loss of his ring, this scene ends with Gratiano's similar discomfort *imminent*.

V   *Belmont* (20 minutes). All that is imminent at the end of the play is the traditional comedic prospect of joyful copulation.

Twentieth-century theatre practice has allowed us to rediscover the exquisite timing of Shakespeare's plotting of *The Merchant of Venice*. It has not, however, recovered the play for Antonio. Shylock's theft remains an unsolved crime.

AFTERTHOUGHTS

1

How would *you* approach the questions listed by Thomson on page 54, if you were directing a production of *The Merchant of Venice*?

2

Do you consider it legitimate for an actor to introduce unscripted gestures (such as Mansfield's kiss, described on page 59) or unwritten scenes (such as Irving's interpolation, described on page 60)?

3

Does Thomson convince you that Shakespeare's use of 'imminence' in *The Merchant of Venice* is 'perhaps his major achievement' (pages 61–62)?

4

Do you agree with the closing statement of this essay (page 63)?

Susie Campbell

Susie Campbell is Head of English at the North Westminster School. She is the author of several critical studies.

ESSAY

'Is that the law?': Shakespeare's political cynicism in *The Merchant of Venice*

The world of *The Merchant of Venice* is dangerous and uncertain. It is a world of chance, hazard and possible mishap. A fortune can be won or lost on the turn of a tide; the hand of a chosen bride secured or forfeited on the luck of a decision. Moreover, it is a world in which different races and religions sit uneasily with one another and apparent courtesies conceal prejudices and bitter enmities. Greed, extravagance, sexual rivalry and racial hatred combine in a potent mixture of suspicion and plotting. The one safe haven in these turbulent waters is the law. The stability and predictability of Venetian law is the rock to which anxious citizens cling. 'There is no power in Venice/ Can alter a decree establishèd', (IV.1.215–216) affirms Portia (in disguise as Balthasar) in Act IV scene 1 of the play. Tampering with the law would, then, be fatal. It would undermine the state's very foundation stone.

However, Venice's foundations, it seems, are shaky. Its

apparently strict and impartial code can be twisted into an instrument of irrational hatred, used to sanction acts of savage cruelty and, just as damaging to its status as a known and predictable code, manipulated by the legal quibbles of an imposter to produce unexpected and surprising outcomes. Far from being the bedrock of stability it is considered, Venetian law, it seems, is as shifting and uncertain as the lagoons and marshes upon which its economic and material security depend.

And yet, Venetian citizens not only continue to believe in the firmness of their law, but also consider it — with a naïvety not found in first-year law students — synonymous with justice. The whole justice and mercy debate of Act IV is premised on the generally accepted belief that Venetian law and justice are one and the same. Shylock comes to court demanding the law — ironically, it is rarely Shylock himself who uses the term 'justice' — and that is interpreted as a demand for justice. Portia talks to him of 'the justice of thy plea' (IV.1.200) when what she means is the *legality* of the bond. Again, she says:

> For, as thou urgest justice, be assured
> Thou shalt have justice . . .

> (IV.1.312–313)

She adds, 'more than thou desir'st', revealing her own misunderstanding of the concept. To counter the supposed harsh justice of the law, the Duke and Portia plead the cause of mercy. The eloquence of their pleas elevates the legal arguments of the courtroom to a great moral debate that has attracted considerable critical attention. However, my argument in this essay is that this moral debate is highly ironic and serves only to underline the lack of any serious ethical underpinning of the Venetian legal system. The play constantly works, I suggest, to undermine the seriousness and integrity of the law. Furthermore, this cynicism is not just gratuitous but has a political purpose. Shakespeare's cynical treatment of the law had an important contemporary significance.

In his article, 'The Governing Idea' (*Shakespeare Quarterly*, 1, London, 1948), Nevill Coghill urges strongly that the justice–mercy debate is the 'governing idea' or main theme of the play. However, whilst the terms 'justice' and 'mercy' are bandied around a lot in Act IV, I have already begun to suggest that we see precious little of either quality in the play itself. We are wrong to invest the debate with any great significance at all, argues John Palmer. His discussion of the trial as a 'great comic scene' (*Comic Characters of Shakespeare*, London, 1946) suggests that the Duke's and Portia's bids for mercy are misleadingly powerful. In fact, he claims, they should only be seen as necessary steps towards the comic dénouement of Shylock's self-defeat. They are necessary in order to have Shylock refuse to show leniency and insist on the full rigours of the law, only to come to the appalled, comic realisation: 'Is *that* the law?' when it is turned against him. (IV.1.311, my emphasis.) Palmer's view is persuasive, but it does not account for the fact that Shakespeare undeniably gives the justice–mercy debate added significance by setting it in the context of a confrontation between a Christian and a Jew. Irresistibly, the debate gains an added religious and moral resonance. Nor is there much doubt that the play offers Christianity as the better alternative, for all the critical treatment many of the Christian characters in the play receive. Jessica is grateful to Lorenzo for securing her conversion. She says jestingly, but with feeling, to Launcelot:

I shall be saved by my husband. He hath made me a Christian.
(III.5.17–18)

Within this context, the justice–mercy debate reverberates with echoes of the biblical debate between the New Law and the Old, even if the play is not quite the 'allegory' of these things that Coghill suggests.

Shakespeare, then, invests the opposing concepts of Justice and Mercy with significance. However, that significance is primarily dramatic and ironic, rather than moral. The irony of the debate is apparent in the hypocrisy of those who claim to uphold these concepts. Justice, as we have seen, means little more than legal revenge — for Portia as well as for Shylock. Mercy receives no more than lip-service. All those 'Christian' pleas for mercy at the beginning of Act IV give way to most unchristian rejoicing in Shylock's downfall at the end. For sheer malicious spite, even Shylock cannot match Gratiano's response to Portia's advice to 'beg mercy of the Duke':

Beg that thou mayst have leave to hang thyself,

And yet, thy wealth being forfeit to the state,
Thou hast not left the value of a cord,
Therefore thou must be hanged at the state's charge.

(IV.1.361–364)

The Duke himself, who joins Portia in pleading for mercy early on in Act IV, when given the chance to demonstrate this quality, strips Shylock of his whole fortune and means to exist. Ironically, the Duke presents this harsh judgement as an act of Christian mercy:

That thou shalt see the difference of our spirit,
I pardon thee thy life before thou ask it.
For half thy wealth, it is Antonio's,
The other half comes to the general state,
Which humbleness may drive unto a fine.

(IV.1.365–369)

All the fine speeches made on behalf of justice and mercy, then, only serve to emphasise how far away from such moral concepts is Venetian society, and in particular, its legal system. In fact, the citizens of Venice seem perfectly clear-sighted about what is the real basis for their law. It is not justice nor morality: it is economic interest. The key reason for upholding the letter of the law is to protect commerce. Antonio points out, reasonably:

The Duke cannot deny the course of law,
For the commodity that strangers have
With us in Venice, if it be denied,
Will much impeach the justice of the state,
Since that the trade and profit of the city
Consisteth of all nations.

(III.3.26–31)

As a merchant himself, Antonio understands perfectly that the main reason for Venice's fixed and known legal system is its need to maintain international confidence. Venetian law is based not on moral concepts but economic and mercantile interest. Shylock also understands this perfectly well. He reminds the court of what is at stake if it does not uphold his bond:

If you deny it, let the danger light

Upon your charter and your city's freedom!

(IV.1.38–39)

And again:

If you deny me, fie upon your law!
There is no force in the decrees of Venice.

(IV.1.101–102)

In *The Merchant of Venice*, then, the law is presented cynically. Its relationship with high-flown concepts such as justice and mercy is ironic. No less cynical is the play's treatment of legal procedure. Shylock's replies to the Duke in the trial-scene reveal his total contempt for the proceedings of the courtroom:

You'll ask me why I rather choose to have
A weight of carrion flesh than to receive
Three thousand ducats. I'll not answer that,
But say it is my humour. Is it answered?

(IV.1.40–43)

But this lack of respect is warranted by the game of verbal skills the legal process is shown to be. Far from being a fair, impartial judicial system, the law in Venice is a battle of wits. Bassanio exposes the lack of objectivity in the legal process when, at Belmont, he muses on the world's gullibility:

The world is still deceived with ornament.
In law, what plea so tainted and corrupt,
But being seasoned with a gracious voice,
Obscures the show of evil?

(III.2.74–77)

Portia defeats Shylock at the trial simply because she is a more skilful player at this particular game. As Balthasar, she sways the court's judgement with a quibble over precise legality that unwittingly exposes the law as a game of interpretation and construction that owes nothing to the concept of justice:

This bond doth give thee here no jot of blood;
The words expressly are 'a pound of flesh'.
Take then thy bond, take thou thy pound of flesh,

But in the cutting it if thou dost shed
One drop of Christian blood, thy lands and goods
Are by the laws of Venice confiscate
Unto the state of Venice.

(IV.1.303–309)

Moreover, this winning stroke is played by an imposter. Portia is no lawyer, but a prankster in disguise. Palmer argues that this whole scene is meant to be fantastic, merely part of the whole 'tall tale' of the play. Nevertheless, it is significant that Portia's disguise, part of the love-game she plays with Bassanio, extends to the courtroom. The play thus undermines the seriousness and weightiness of the law and the courtroom.

There is an interesting parallel between what happens in the courtroom and what happens at Belmont. The choice of the correct chest at Belmont is supposed to be a matter of judgement, a test set by Portia's father to ensure that she marries a man of integrity and wisdom. Nerissa appreciates this when she says optimistically that she 'will no doubt never be chosen by any rightly but one who you shall rightly love' (I.2.30–31). Portia seems rather more pessimistic, for all that she holds herself bound by her father's will:

I may neither choose who I would nor refuse who I dislike, so is the will of a living daughter curbed by the will of a dead father.

(I.2.22–24)

Significantly, the whole task of choosing the right casket is surrounded by imagery of chance and hazard so that it seems more a lottery than a test of wise judgement. Portia attempts to postpone Bassanio's choice, urging him, 'I pray you tarry, pause a day or two/ Before you hazard' (III.2.1–2), and 'I would detain you here some month or two/ Before you venture for me'. (III.2.9–10). Her anxious, 'if he lose' (III.2.44) is more appropriate for a player in a game of chance than a man confronted with a question for wise judgement. Even after Bassanio makes his choice and ably proves his ability to make sound decisions, he refers to himself as the winning player in a sporting event: 'Like one of two contending in a prize' (III.2.141) is how he describes himself. Nor is this game of wit and skill without its foundation in commercial interest. Whilst Bassanio protests his love for

70

where

Portia, his original motive for seeking her hand was to recover his fortune. The worlds of Venice and Belmont are more closely linked than they might appear. If sordid financial interest infiltrates the beautiful and harmonious world of Belmont, equally alarmingly the games and teasing wars of words, appropriate to courtship, prevail in Venice's courtroom.

Our confidence in Portia's integrity as a lawyer is undermined by the lighthearted way in which she undertakes her disguise. She sets out to ridicule the habits of a young man:

> I have within my mind
> A thousand raw tricks of these bragging Jacks
> Which I will practise.
>
> (III.4.76–78)

She describes her plan to go to Venice in disguise as a lawyer as a 'device' (III.4.81), a mere trick or prank. This comic levity is restrained during the actual court scene but bursts out again immediately afterwards in the scene during which she tricks Bassanio out of his ring. The whole episode seems like an exuberant escapade to Portia. Whilst this is in keeping with the play's comic intent, it nevertheless adds to the play's erosion of any serious belief in the gravity of the legal process.

On the one hand, then, there is the eloquent and high-minded debate about justice and mercy. On the other, there is the law itself. Founded on commercial interest and open to manipulation by the verbally adept, the law is exposed as a pragmatic, man-made system of rules and regulations. But this is no mere cynicism. Shakespeare's treatment of the law in this play has a wider significance.

If the law lacks any real moral authority, then why shouldn't the Duke, as ruler of the state, overturn it where it seems desirable? Some characters in the play seem to think that he could or should do this. Solanio says to Antonio:

> I am sure the Duke
> Will never grant this forfeiture to hold.
>
> (III.3.24–25)

And Bassanio urges the court:

> Wrest once the law to your authority,

> To do a great right, do a little wrong
>
> (IV.1.212–213)

However, Portia, Shylock, Antonio and the Duke himself are all adamant that this cannot be. However bizarre the outcome, the law must be upheld in every particular. This insistence on the priority of the law combines with the way that the play continually works to undermine the credibility of this same law to produce an interesting result. The Duke, who declares himself subordinate to the law, turns into a curiously impotent figure. At the beginning of Act IV, the Duke's efforts to persuade Shylock to show clemency have already been flouted and ignored. The best he can offer Antonio is ineffectual sympathy. When Shylock himself appears, we actually see the Duke go through the humiliating process of pleading with him yet again to show mercy. Their positions are reversed: the Duke is in the position of petitioner while Shylock is the one in a powerful position. With legality on his side, Shylock can snap his fingers in the Duke's face. Antonio was right: 'The Duke cannot deny the course of law' (III.3.26).

The dramatic presentation of a ruler helpless before the law would have had tremendous contemporary significance. Throughout the sixteenth and seventeenth centuries, the relationship of a ruler to the law was hotly disputed, culminating, of course, in the great constitutional crisis of the seventeenth century. Historian Christopher Hill has repeatedly stressed the centrality of the law to all the political and constitutional debates of this era. Men 'thought in legal terms', he insists in *The Century of Revolution* (London, 1961). The key legal issue was whether the sovereign was above the law or bound by its dictates like everyone else. Throughout Elizabeth I's reign and on into the reigns of her successors, this issue was unsettled. Shakespeare, of course, does not contribute directly to this debate. What he does give us is a powerful dramatic sense of a ruler whose authority is diminished because he holds himself subordinate to the law, and a cynical undermining of any notion that the law has any moral authority beyond its social and economic basis. Interestingly, in contrast with the Duke as a figure of limited power, the figure of a king, when evoked by Portia, is invested with almost divine attributes:

72

> But mercy is above this sceptred sway,
> It is enthronèd in the hearts of kings,
> It is an attribute to God himself
>
> (IV.1.190–192)

By emphasising the moral bankruptcy of the law and the impotence of a ruler bound by it, Shakespeare helps to prepare the ground for a theory of sovereign power as above the law, a political theory which was to be fully articulated and fought over in the next century. In many of his later plays, Shakespeare returns to the question of a ruler's relationship to the law and looks at it from different aspects, but in *The Merchant of Venice* the cynical treatment of the law seems to have clear political implications.

In 1605, *The Merchant of Venice* was presented to James I at court. He liked it so much that he commanded a second performance on the following Tuesday. James I, the chief architect of the theory of the divine right of kings, clearly found something in the play that pleased his political palate.

AFTERTHOUGHTS

1

What distinction do you see between 'justice' and 'the law' (page 66)?

2

Does Campbell persuade you that 'the law is presented cynically' in *The Merchant of Venice* (page 69)?

3

What parallels does Campbell identify between the courtroom scene and the scene where Bassanio chooses the right casket (pages 70–71)?

4

What do you think James I might particularly have enjoyed in *The Merchant of Venice* (page 73)?

Christopher McCullough

Christopher McCullough is Lecturer in Drama at the University of Exeter. He is editor of the journal Studies in Theatre Production.

ESSAY

'So shines a good deed in a naughty world' (V.1.91)

The Merchant of Venice, like a number of Shakespeare's other plays, presents problems today because of the distance that separates us from the world picture represented in the play. This distance is manifest not just in terms of historical time (the plays were written a long time ago), nor because they are written in an unfamiliar language. The problem is more often to be located in our reading of the version of reality being promoted by the play. The conventions by which a restrictive status quo is constructed in the sixteenth and seventeenth centuries are less likely to go unchallenged today when particular groups of people — such as women or minority ethnic groups — are struggling to gain a voice in our society. The response of many critics and directors is to marginalise such issues by declaring that while certain views may be expressed by characters in the play, this in itself does not make a play reactionary. This of course may be so. Scholars often vindicate Shakespeare's position by referring to his 'universality'. This means that the values represented in his plays reveal eternal truths regarding human nature. His characters speak out across the generations, and their failings as human beings are not products of historical circumstance, but the timeless failings (or indeed virtues) of 'human nature'. The view of reality represented in the play is therefore to be taken as a permanent and unchanging truth.

This kind of reading may lead us to suppose that Shylock's behaviour has little to do with the fact that he is a Jew living under duress in an intolerant Christian society (I.3.94–134). A conventional reading — certainly paramount in the work of John Barton (*Playing Shakespeare*, London, 1984) — is that Shylock is simply a bad human being. That he is Jewish and essentially a lone Jew ranged against the Christian society does not, in Barton's analysis, make the play anti-semitic. The other two Jews — Tubal and Jessica — do not figure in this opposition in the same way. This of course may be considered as a valid argument, but only if we remove the play from any form of historical contextualisation and overlook a substantial amount of evidence derived from the making of the play through its stage history. All the evidence points to the supposition that until the 1740s (we have little information on the nature of the original performance) the character of Shylock was a part for low comedians. The likelihood is that rather than this being a convention by which the comedian achieved a sympathetic and conspiratorial relationship with the audience, it was a means to distance and ridicule the alien about whom little was known, but much feared. This was a common occurrence then as now. Regard the burning in effigy of grotesque caricatures that represent hated figures: any current president of the United States of America, Salman Rushdie, Guy Fawkes! Certainly the thesis that Shylock was a Pantalone comic figure taken from the Italian *commedia dell'arte* (experience of which may have been Shakespeare's insight into aspects of Venetian life) is historically faulty though the fault may be Shakespeare's rather than his interpreters. Pantalone was a merchant and in sixteenth-century Venice Jews were not allowed to undertake trade as merchants. Their means of livelihood was restricted to the profession of usurer; as of course is Shylock's.

In the late eighteenth and nineteenth centuries 'serious' actors undertook the role of interpreting Shylock in a more tragic mode. However, one of the distinctions between literary and theatrical signification is the visual dimension. The 'tragic' interpretations of John Philip Kemble and Charles Macklin, amongst other notables, carried with them the visual codes of grotesque alien features derived from the stereotypical assumptions associated with the effigy that symbolises the fear of the unknown. The rendering of Shylock as a tragic figure threatening the 'comic' figures of the play had little to do with the concept of 'tragic' meaning pity and more to do with 'tragic' meaning terror. Critics of the eighteenth century saw more of a savage fierceness and spirit of revenge than they did an object of pity. Even Kean, whose interpretation of the part was more sympathetic than many, achieved his sympathy by robbing Shylock of his Jewishness and declaring him, in his behaviour, to be more than half Christian. The consequence of this interpretation meant presumably that Shylock appeared to be more 'human'. The analysis offered by contemporary critics as exemplified by John Barton, suggests that humanity, rather than being a social construct, is a quality like mercy that drops, 'as the gentle rain from heaven' (IV.1.182). Kean's analysis suggests that Shylock's 'humanity' may be acquired by adoption of his antagonists' religion. Nowhere is there a suggestion that Christianity in this context is a question of spiritual conversion. Every reference in this direction follows the pattern of 'Two things provided more: that for this favour/ He presently become a Christian' (IV.1.383–384).

Shylock is arguably the character by which the play is best known, but he is not the only figure of complexity. The 'naughty world' of this play is a world where we may pursue, with some justification, the thesis that all the oppressed are also oppressors. Shylock may well be a victim of how Jews have been constructed in the popular imagination, but he also engenders good reason for disliking him. The other main characters in The Merchant of Venice exhibit the same ambiguity. To be a Christian in the play does not mean that you behave in a 'Christian' way. Neville Coghill's view that the play is an allegory of the old law and the new — the Old and New Testaments — (Shakespeare Quarterly, 1, Cambridge, 1948) does not hold much credence when we examine the attitudes of Venice and Belmont. If the Jew Shylock is meant to represent the old law, and the Christians in the play the new law, there are problems. The law in one way or another is a central issue, but the characters do not quite fit the pattern of the supposed allegory. Shylock may well correspond to an Old Testament concept of revenge, but the Christians hardly represent the values taught in the New Testament. It is the law of property that has priority rather than any idea of a spiritual law of charity. Indeed we may go further and say that people are regarded primarily for their cash value as embodied in commodities such as caskets, argosies and jewels.

The social patterning of the play places Shylock in isolation against the two major figures of Antonio and Portia. The other characters in the play occupy roles that range between these three figures both in dramatic importance and social status. No single person may be said to be blameless in this predatory world where human life is measured and quantified by the yardstick of the cash value of commodities. Between the poles of Antonio/Portia and their antagonist Shylock exists a complex pattern of status based on deceit and the oppression of oppressors. Of particular note are Jessica, Lorenzo, Nerissa, Gratiano, the Gobbos and Bassanio.

Our first meeting with both Antonio and Portia is disconcerting. Even the slightest prior acquaintance with the play usually informs us that it is Portia who has the most famous lines in the play. So often the cultural power of a play by Shakespeare relies, initially, upon the currency of the famous lines from that particular play. In *Hamlet*, arguably the most famous play by Britain's most famous writer, many lines have become public property: 'To be, or not to be' (III.1.56), or the misquotation, 'Alas, poor Yorick! I knew him well' (V.1.182). Portia we know by 'The quality of mercy is not strained,' (IV.1.181) and that knowledge presumes the fullness of the remarkable young woman who takes on the might and authority of Venetian law in order to defeat the savage revenge of Shylock. Further study of the play enables us to ask certain questions about the verity of this construction of Portia's character. Our first meeting is, as it is in the case of Antonio, with an individual who is bored with life. Portia displays the qualities we often associate with an over-privileged life-style, 'By my troth, Nerissa, my little body is aweary of this great world' (I.2.1–2). She is not weary from labour but from frustration at the conditions of her father's will. Any sympathy for this predicament is tempered by Nerissa's response which immediately takes Portia to task by contextualising her 'misery' in lines 3–9. Portia's status is complex. She is both an oppressor and oppressed. The conditions of her father's will are to our eyes intolerable, yet the bigotry displayed in Portia's attitude to her potential suitors undermines the popular signification of 'the quality of mercy'. Quite apart from the cultural stereotyping of the suitors in Act I scene 2, the clear racism of her attitude towards the Prince of Morocco sets the scene for her compliance with the general attitudes of the 'Christians' towards Shylock: 'If he have the condition of a saint and the complexion of a devil, I had rather he should shrive me than wive me' (I.2.123–125) — the 'complexion of a devil' meaning that he is black. Portia is trapped in her luxury by the will of one man while at the same time dismissing her potential suitors on the grounds of their race. Her condition is of course further complicated by the fact that no matter what she thinks of any individual suitor, she is impotently bound by their choice of the appropriate casket to marry one of them.

Portia's greatest moment of power comes in her handling of the law. Her guise as the young doctor is intriguing. Why does Portia need, if she has the skill to acquire the expertise of a doctor of laws, to disguise herself? (That she accomplishes this with such speed and apparent ease may suggest that Shakespeare had a low opinion of lawyers!) Or we may surmise that she has the intention to further prove her husband's character and fidelity, as is seen in the saga of the rings at the end of the trial and in Act V. This is a pretty thin argument. More likely is the fact that social constraints on what a woman may or may not accomplish in public are the reasons behind the necessity for disguise. Again the pattern of power and constraint is exercised, as it is with her wealth and her father's decree on her marriage. Many people, whether they are critics or members of audiences, find the actual outcome of the trial a discomforting experience. It can't just be put down to a slight unease at the harsh judgement of the Duke after Portia's legal victory. To rely solely on that aspect would certainly suggest rampant anti-semitism. As Terry Eagleton points out (*William Shakespeare*, Oxford, 1986, pp. 35–48), Portia's reading of the law is 'true to the text but therefore lamentably false to its meaning'. Eagleton's argument rests upon an understanding of the law as necessarily being general in its linguistic structure. That is to be 'independent of and indifferent to any concrete situation'. The outcome otherwise would mean that we would need laws for every specific situation. Judgements in courts of law are expected to be in the 'spirit' of the law, drawing on an acceptable common sense according to the particular legal context. Eagleton's argument on Portia's interpretation of the law follows the line that she is too 'crassly literal' and that her quibbling over the spilling of Christian blood would be ruled out of order in a modern court. His view is that Shylock has 'forced the Christians into outdoing his own *inhuman* legalism'. The status quo of male Christian hierarchy is only maintained by the legalistic pedantry of one who paradoxically, despite ingenuity and wealth, is herself under considerable constraint. The subsequent duping of Bassanio and Gratiano into parting with the rings given to them by their newly 'acquired' wives functions as a mild mirror to what may be seen as Shylock's 'victory' in the trial. Briefly Portia shares a similarly alienated position with Shylock. They both, from their marginalised social roles, achieve a covert act of subversion against those who seek to constrain them.

Antonio is of course the 'merchant' of Venice, but for one who is so central to the play's iconography, he is a curiously passive figure. Our meeting with him in the first speech of the play indicates a similarly languid mood to that which we perceive in Portia. 'In sooth I know not why I am so sad./ It wearies me, you say it wearies you' (I.1.1–2). That Antonio is melancholic is obvious to all, and that his melancholia is without (at least in this scene) obvious cause is typical of the neurosis. He seems well fitted to take his place alongside other well-known Shakespearean melancholics like Jaques in *As You Like It*. Jaques even echoes Antonio's lines in melancholia: 'A stage where every man must play a part' (I.1.78) — although perhaps the lines are even closer to the later play *Macbeth* ('Life's but a walking shadow, a poor player/ That struts and frets his hour upon the stage', V.5.24–25). Macbeth, however, has more pressing problems than the loss of argosies or lovers. In one sense Antonio has all that his antagonist Shylock does not have. His status in the Venetian hierarchy of merchants is secure financially and it is clear from the very outset that he has a close circle of friends. His divorce from purpose and the emptiness upon which his melancholia feeds is already well established. His priority in establishing value to his argosies is not based on the usefulness of his cargo, but merely on its profit potential. Antonio alienates the products of his economic activity in the form of money and capital. This in itself provides the necessary void and sense of dislocation from practical values that motivates the melancholia. In this Antonio and Shylock bear an unlikely similarity to one another. Antonio by the circumstances of his profession is constructed in an ideological paradigm wherein he, by separating use from value, becomes divorced from purpose. Thus, within his own consciousness, he experiences self-alienation.

Shylock, by the circumstance of his race and culture, is discriminated against and marginalised by the Christian hegemony. The only profession open to him is that of usurer, a lender of money for the profit accrued through interest rates on repayment. It is a profession that depends upon an ideology that assigns an intrinsic value to money. His wealth depends upon money being able to engender money. He is alienated both by and from the culture that has determined the only profession he is allowed to pursue. This in its turn brings about a form of self-alienation in his relationship with the one person who should be closest to him: Jessica. Antonio's melancholy may be seen to be an indulgence in self-absorption; Shylock's alienation carries with it the real danger of physical persecution. The seeds of this persecution are seen in the daily physical abuse poured upon Shylock by Antonio. 'Fair sir, you spat on me on Wednesday last,/ You spurned me such a day, another time/ You called me dog' (I.3.123–125). It is this physical and cultural abuse that fuels Shylock's motivation for revenge upon Antonio.

In a culture that divorces use from value it is only logical for that principle to be carried one stage further. Thus, it is doubtful whether we could argue the case for any one character being valued wholly for his or her humanity. There is sufficient evidence to point to Portia's commodity value in terms of her wealth being a primary motivation in Bassanio's mind. Whatever the relationship between Antonio and Bassanio has been, Antonio, once Bassanio has Portia in his sights, has a value in the capital he can provide for the young entrepreneur's venture to Belmont. It is obvious that no one in the Christian society of Venice would think of approaching Shylock were it not for the fact that he possesses a commodity value in ready cash. Even Jessica may be seen in terms of her stolen 'dowry'. The objectification of human beings almost exclusively in terms of money is apposite to the value systems already discussed. However, it is ironical that the bond that Shylock demands is not in the form of cash interest or even property, but in the shape of Antonio himself, or at least a portion of him! A perverse circle has been turned. The use value of objects has been supplanted by their monetary value. The value of people for their humanity has been dislocated by their immediate value as financial assets. But now the human body has become the ultimate commodity. Even money is placed secondary to this object as we see when Shylock only considers taking three times the amount he loaned to Antonio when it is clear that he has lost his case in court. But what value does a pound of Antonio's flesh possess? Obviously none in terms of the open market, unless people are turning to cannibalism. The only value is in the strength of Shylock's desire for revenge. The human body, so far removed from humanity in this play, has now achieved the power to fuel and satiate human emotions; it has become reunited with 'humanity', but in a most grotesque version created by inhumane social conditions.

The dilemma of societies like Venice and Belmont may be summed up in Launcelot Gobbo's dilemma, as he seeks to leave the service of Shylock. He describes himself as placed between his 'conscience' and 'the fiend' (II.1.1–28). Here is a clown (unlike early stage presentations of Shylock) who may achieve a degree of complicity with the audience through his recognition of the 'naughty world' represented on stage.

AFTERTHOUGHTS

1

Is it valid to consider a play without reference to its historical context?

2

What is your explanation for Portia's use of disguise (page 79)?

3

Do you agree with McCullough's account of Antonio's 'self-alienation' (page 81)?

4

What do you understand by 'a culture that divorces use from value' (page 81)?

Angus Alton

Angus Alton works as a researcher for the University of Oxford Delegacy of Local Examinations. He is also an experienced examiner in English Literature at GCSE and A level.

ESSAY

The importance of the main plot in *The Merchant of Venice*

Those familiar with examination questions on Shakespeare, and especially those studying *King Lear*, will recognise the source of the title of this essay. It is generally assumed that the plays possess a high level of structural unity, and therefore that events not directly a part of the main plot should help to further our understanding of the themes and issues in the play. Thus, a standard topic for consideration is how any sub-plots fit into the ideas handled in the main plot of a play. It seems a reasonable question to ask, especially when, as in *King Lear*, parallels between events in the various plots are often made explicit in the text.

However, as the inversion of expectations in my title implies, *The Merchant of Venice* presents something of a paradox from this point of view. For a variety of reasons — some of them psychological, some theatrical and some historical — most of the interest of modern audiences, actors, producers and critics focuses on Shylock and what our attitude to him should be. This has long been the case, even in ages which were much less concerned with issues like anti-semitism, but clearly the Holocaust has given especial emphasis and poignancy to the treatment of Shylock. As a result, for many people whose acquaintance with the play is relatively casual, the assumption is that the title of the play refers to the Jewish money-lender rather than his most bitter enemy, Antonio, the real merchant.

Yet, structurally, the story of Shylock's 'merry bond' (I.3.170) is very much secondary to that of Bassanio's search for his personal 'golden fleece' (I.1.70), sponsored by Antonio. The one is, after all, wholly dependent on the other, for without Bassanio's need for money with which to finance his quest, there would be no need for Antonio to seal the bond. Moreover, the question of the pound of flesh is resolved by the end of Act IV scene 1, leaving more than a whole Act in which other matters are dealt with. (One is reminded of *Macbeth*, in which Shakespeare, having created a Lady Macbeth who draws much of our attention in the first half of the play, almost eliminates her from the second half, and leaves Macbeth virtually a whole Act in which to come to terms with his own situation alone.)

To be fair, the main plot–sub-plot division in *The Merchant of Venice* is not quite as clear-cut as implied in the preceding paragraph. In a sense, the story of Bassanio's quest is concluded even sooner than that of the bond: when he chooses the correct casket in Act III scene 2. The ring episode is in no way integral to the question of Bassanio's choice, and, indeed, can be seen as arising more from Portia's part in Shylock's story than from anything else. Further, the significant part that Lorenzo and Jessica play in establishing the mood of the final scene provides a sharp reminder that Shylock has lost his daughter as well as his ducats. It is hard to resist the conclusion that the final Act has little function other than to dispel the disturbing aftertaste of the courtroom scene, which would seem to suggest that the tendency to focus on Shylock, and the question of the fairness of his treatment, is by no means mistaken.

In this context, it is worth noting that the title of the play, although it doesn't refer to Shylock, is not, say, 'Bassanio and Portia' or 'The Caskets'. Instead it refers to the character who unites the two strands, but who is otherwise rather nebulous and elusive. Significantly, he is a rather isolated figure onstage at the end as the other characters pair off—an aspect I shall return to later on.

Quite which is the main plot of *The Merchant of Venice* is, then, arguable, and there is little point in seeking to resist the forces of history. What is not arguable, however, is that the events involving Bassanio and Portia tend to be comparatively neglected, and, using the assumption outlined in the opening paragraph, it would seem desirable, at the very least, to consider to what extent they may help to inform our understanding of those involving Shylock.

In this respect, the structure of the play is very important, and it is an aspect which will be explored fully later on. For the moment I would like to focus on the way the opening scenes of the play immediately establish parallels between the two plots. The use of Antonio as the title character of the play is an important element in this, for it focuses our attention not on Bassanio or Shylock, but on their relationship with Antonio. On the surface, Bassanio comes out of the comparison well, for Antonio's attitude to him is open and positive, while the initial coldness and downright hostility between Shylock and Antonio creates immediate unease. Moreover, the mistrust that Bassanio expresses at the close of Act I scene 3 serves to heighten that unease.

In the event, of course, that superficial impression is proved correct, but that should not lead us to assume it *is* correct, or, rather, that it is correct for the right reasons. The opening scenes which introduce us to plot, character and themes are, in fact, sufficiently subtle and complex to deserve rather more careful consideration. There are, for example, grounds for some very real reservations about Bassanio's character as we see it in the very first scene. For a start, there is the fact that he has, by his own admission:

> disabled mine estate
> By something showing a more swelling port
> Than my faint means would grant continuance.

(I.1.123–125)

This, though, is something that his admission mitigates, and is anyway in the awkward area of factors necessary for the plot to occur at all, which it is unwise to use in character analysis. Two interrelated points are, however, less excusable. The first is the fact that, in his account of Portia and his suit for her, he omits to mention the caskets, instead optimistically declaring:

> I have a mind presages me such thrift
> That I should questionless be fortunate.
>
> (I.1.175–176)

It seems implausible to claim that he is himself ignorant of the terms of Portia's father's will, since it implies that she must have concealed them from him. Anyway, the audience is informed of the will in the very next scene, which inevitably colours our response to the signing of the bond. Then there is the matter of the order Bassanio chooses when he rehearses Portia's qualities: first Antonio is told she is 'richly left', then that she is 'fair' and only then that she is 'of wondrous virtues' (all I.1.161–163). Even if we accept that this is in order to build to a climax, it is hard not to suspect *at this stage* that Portia's fortune is at least a major factor in Bassanio's attraction to her; worse, he may be emphasising the financial element in order to appeal to Antonio's mercantile instincts, and if so this suggests a disturbing lack of openness on his part.

Conversely, Shylock's behaviour is comparatively open. It is true that the fullness of his hatred is only expressed in his aside, warning us:

> If I can catch him once upon the hip,
> I will feed fat the ancient grudge I bear him.
>
> (I.3.43–44)

(And the monosyllables and alliterated f's underline the intensity of the emotion.) There is, then, clearly insincerity in his claim 'I would be friends with you' (I.3.135), but he makes no secret of the grounds of that 'ancient grudge'. The eloquent speech in which he outlines the wrongs done to him and his 'tribe' (I.3.103–126) is at the least a powerful warning about the likely state of his feelings. It is true that Shylock probably has the underlying intention in the speech of embarrassing Antonio, and perhaps subtly forcing him to accept the terms of the loan. If this is so, it can hardly be said to work, for Antonio's reply is wholly unrepentant:

> I am as like to call thee so again,
> To spit on thee again, to spurn thee too.
>
> (I.3.127–128)

Bassanio, too, is unimpressed and seeks to dissuade Antonio from signing the bond. There is, anyway, a more demanding issue in this scene than the question of Shylock's motivation in rehearsing Antonio's insults: it is that of Shylock's motivation in the bond he proposes. It is most unlikely that a successful money-lender like Shylock does not know as well as Antonio that the merchant expects 'return/ Of thrice three times the value of this bond' (I.3.155–156). Unless one is to assume that Shylock is somehow — i.e. diabolically — informed that all Antonio's projects are to miscarry (a view which, presumably, rather settles the question of whether we are to sympathise with Shylock) it is hard to see quite what he hopes to gain by his device. At best, he might feel he would gain the moral high ground in his battle against Antonio; but, as we have already heard, Antonio is unlikely to be over-concerned by this, and, anyway, it is hard to regard such an achievement as 'feeding fat' his grudge.

At the beginning of the play, then, the audience has at least some grounds for reservations about Bassanio's honesty, and is in two minds as to whether Shylock has grown kind or is merely offering 'fair terms' but with 'a villain's mind' (I.3.176). Clearly, only the events involving Shylock and Antonio can answer the latter question, but those involving Bassanio can help us not only to clarify our view of him, but also to develop our understanding of what exactly is required to be 'kind'.

In this context, the fairy-tale nature of the caskets means that, to some extent at least, tension is absent from the story: the sophisticated audience can almost certainly guess which is the correct casket, and probably assumes that the first two to choose will get it wrong so that we can know what they contain. There is probably not even much doubt that Bassanio will be the one to get it right (although it can certainly be argued that there has been little evidence up to that point that the play is a comedy). Instead, the audience is largely free to consider the lessons that the caskets contain, lessons which, as with many fairy-tales, are profoundly moral in nature. They are also closely connected with our understanding of the bond and Shylock's behaviour in the courtroom scene.

In the first instance, it can reasonably be assumed that the other suitors are given — albeit sketchily — characters which help us to grasp what is going on. Thus, it is no surprise that Morocco, who talks of having a 'golden mind' (II.7.20), should choose the golden casket. Moreover, there is an important irony that his first speech in the play should urge Portia to look behind the surface of his complexion, yet it is he who should assume that Portia is 'what many men desire', and he who needs to be reminded that *'All that glisters is not gold'* (II.7.65), which is essentially the obverse of the truth that he initially insisted on. He is, in a sense, dead to the real meaning of looking beneath the surface of things, and thus it is appropriate that this casket should contain a 'carrion Death' (II.7.63) to tell him that *'[his] suit is cold'* (II.7.73) just as he is.

By the same token, it is hard not to believe that Shakespeare has chosen the Prince of Arragon as the second suitor as much for the phonic resonance of his name as for any other reason. He is able to resist the lure of the golden casket only because he does not want to ally himself with 'the fool multitude' (II.9.26) and instead he 'assume[s] desert' (II.9.51). That he deserves the 'portrait of a blinking idiot' (II.9.54) is evidenced as much by the fact that he refuses to accept his fate ('Are my deserts no better?', II.9.60) and needs to be reminded by Portia that:

> To offend and judge are distinct offices,
> And of opposèd natures.
>
> (II.9.61–62)

I do not wish to extend the analysis of the unsuccessful suitors too far: there is little character detail to justify more than the minor observations above. Indeed, their similarities are almost as important as any differences: neither rejects the other wrong casket with any real conviction (Morocco, too, feels he deserves Portia) and, significantly, neither experiences any difficulty in rejecting the lead casket. It is this which should inform our response when Bassanio is making his choice. It is worth noting at this point that Arragon is in a sense correct in his reason for rejecting the gold casket. Although we now know that 'what many men desire' is death, a true appreciation of Portia's worth is not one that 'the fool multitude' can arrive at. Unfortunately for him, he *is* a part of a similar multitude who 'assume desert'.

There is, then, a strong case for resolving doubts about Bassanio in his favour, simply because he chooses the right casket. His reasoning while making that choice only serves to support it. (The question of whether the song is a deliberate ploy to assist Bassanio is irrelevant here: his interior monologue is quite sufficient to enable us to believe that the reasoning is sincere.) It is true that he is assisted to a degree by his character and situation. The extravagant streak in his nature that he outlined in the first scene may make it relatively easy for him to resist the lure of both 'thou gaudy gold' (III.2.101) and of the 'pale and common drudge/ 'Tween man and man' (III.2.103–104). But it could just as easily be argued that it would make him more vulnerable to them. Besides, as has already been pointed out, Morocco, too, has good reason to avoid surface attractiveness. What is more interesting in this context is the possibility that Antonio's willing signing of the bond helps Bassanio to understand the importance of giving and hazarding all he has.

Certainly, there is no denying that Bassanio's speech shows him to be uncannily in tune with Portia's father's ideas. Not only does he realise in general terms that 'The world is still deceived with ornament' (III.2.74), but he specifically associates 'golden locks' (III.2.92) with a skull and the sepulchre (III.2.96). In the same way, he approves the lead casket because 'Thy paleness moves me more than eloquence' (III.2.106), which subtly recalls the message in the silver casket which reminds us that folly can be 'Silvered o'er' (II.9.69). The scroll in the lead casket serves to confirm that Bassanio chooses 'not by the view' (III.2.131) and his actions in the rest of the play are a triumphant affirmation of this.

The idea of not choosing by the view is more than a reminder of the need to look behind surfaces: it emphasises that what matters is not material objects at all. The caskets, far from curbing Portia's choice of husband, have only served to confirm the judgement of her heart. Thus, feelings are valued above such aspects as 'birth', 'fortunes', 'graces' and 'qualities of breeding' (all II.7.32–33), and Bassanio shows that his feelings consistently outweigh any material or temporal considerations. He has no hesitation in postponing the celebration of his marriage on receiving news of Antonio's plight. (It is significant in this context that Antonio's letter stresses that Bassanio must be moved by love in his response if it is to have any meaning.) For the one is a real need of friendship, while the other is ultimately only a material token, which love can dispense with if necessary.

The ring episode, which makes up what one might call the after-plot of the play, further develops this notion. The ring, like the celebration of a marriage, has important symbolic value. The nature of that value is made abundantly clear as Portia gives the ring to Bassanio: to part with the ring is to 'presage the ruin of your love' (III.2.173). Ultimately, however, a ring can do no such thing, and a contest between the need to affirm Bassanio's gratitude on his friend's behalf and the desire to retain a ring which he knows does not affect his feelings for Portia is no contest at all, however much the outcome serves to embarrass him.

Constantly, then, this half of the play demonstrates the primacy of feelings over what is material. The question now is to what extent this issue helps us to respond appropriately to the other story within the play. Before exploring this fully, it is important to stress what is meant by feelings. For in this play, as in most of Shakespeare's plays, emotions are positive rather than negative: hatred tends to seek rational explanations and to suggest that the actions that arise from it are justified. Portia, however, states simply that 'I never did repent for doing good' (III.4.10), offering no real attempt at explanation.

Looking at the events involving Shylock, we can appreciate the full poignancy of them. Instead of seeing him as the victim, requiring our pity, which is a common post-Holocaust way of reading the text, we can view him as very much the villain, but one who is more than worthy of our sympathy. The key here is that the way Shylock is portrayed in the play lets us know that he is alive to the value of the immaterial, the spiritual, but that, for reasons which we can understand if not accept, he chooses his own version of a 'carrion Death'.

It is probably no accident that a key moment in revealing to us Shylock's potential should also involve a ring. When Tubal brings news of Jessica's exchange of a ring for a monkey, Shylock's anguished cry is:

> It was my turquoise; I had it of Leah when I was a bachelor. I would not have given it for a wilderness of monkeys.
>
> (III.1.110–113)

He too knows that there are items which completely transcend their material value. What is more, his use of the key term 'kind' when offering the bond (I.3.139) shows that he is aware that there is an important dimension to human relationships which derives from our shared humanity. This is also evidenced by what is probably his most famous speech in the play: '. . . Hath not a Jew eyes? . . . If you prick us, do we not bleed? . . .' (III.1.53–59).

However, a mixture of grievance arising from a sense that others have slighted his humanity ('You call me misbeliever, cut-throat dog', I.3.108) coupled with despair arising from the loss of the last thing which might affirm his humanity, his daughter, causes Shylock to opt for what is material and what is negative. The process is already well under way when the play opens: for him, only his gold now breeds (I.3.93) and it is clear that Jessica is seen more as a possession than as a person. What the play shows is how corrosive the power of hatred can be, once it is indulged. There is something horrible in the fact that in the very scene when he attests the value of his ring — or rather its pricelessness — he can also say: 'I would my daughter were dead at my foot, and the jewels in her ear!' (III.1.80–81).

Such an inversion of values, however extreme the provocation, shows that there can be no real hope of redemption for Shylock. It comes as no surprise, therefore, that he is so implacable in the courtroom scene. It is important to understand how far Portia's appeals to Shylock fit into this way of looking at the play. She begs him to act in the spirit of the law — i.e. a reading which depends on an irrational and emotional level — rather than its letter. He refuses. She appeals to the ultimately irrational emotion, mercy, which is 'enthronèd in the hearts of kings' (IV.1.191). He is deaf to it. She even seeks to kick start his dormant emotions, by underlining the full consequences of enforcing the bond:

> Have by some surgeon, Shylock, on your charge,
> To stop his wounds, lest he do bleed to death.
>
> (IV.1.254–255)

Shylock will have none of it. Only then does Portia use his own weapon against him, and show how the letter of the law and, hence, *all* rationalism are double-edged weapons at best and can be turned against those who deny their better feelings.

This is not to argue that the treatment meted out to Shylock at the end of the scene is justified, nor that there is no justification for his bitterness. Rather it is to suggest that our sympathy for Shylock is only valid if we fully understand where his fault lies. When we do, we can see how the play is structured: two characters between whom there is little to choose at the outset save that one is motivated by love and the other by hatred are shown in relationship with a common linking figure. The two histories then mirror each other, with both characters seeming to achieve their quest. But the love quest is seen as enabling, while the pursuit of hatred is finally disabling. Shylock is left wholly derelict, while Bassanio has all he could wish. Interestingly, Antonio, who assuredly knows the value of friendship, and the worthlessness of money:

> . . . for when did friendship take
> A breed of barren metal of his friend?

(I.3.130–131)

is nevertheless a merchant, who necessarily depends upon that 'pale and common drudge', money. And, at the end of the play, while he can perhaps bask in the warmth of the general happiness that he has helped to bring about, he is essentially alone, save for his 'argosies' which are 'richly come to harbour' (V.1.276–277). Perhaps that causeless sadness of his with which the play opens, rather than being a precursor of his plight in the course of the play, derives from the emptiness of his life altogether.

AFTERTHOUGHTS

1

Do you agree that 'the final Act has little function other than to dispel the disturbing aftertaste of the courtroom scene' (page 85)?

2

Why do you think Bassanio neglects to mention the caskets when borrowing money from Antonio (pages 86–87)?

3

Do you agree that audiences will 'almost certainly guess which is the correct casket' (page 88)? Did you? And, if so, how and at what stage?

4

What links does Alton establish in this essay between the different plot strands of *The Merchant of Venice*?

Ronald Draper

*Ronald Draper is Regius Professor of
Literature at the University of Aberdeen,
and the author of numerous scholarly
publications.*

ESSAY

'This muddy vesture of decay'

There's not the smallest orb which thou beholdest
But in his motion like an angel sings,
Still quiring to the young-eyed cherubins;
Such harmony is in immortal souls,
But whilst this muddy vesture of decay
Doth grossly close it in, we cannot hear it.

(*The Merchant of Venice*, V.1.60–65)

Lorenzo's tribute to the supposed music of the spheres and
its echoing within the souls of men is eloquent testimony to the
beauty of the universe and to the nobility of the role assigned to
the human race. It foreshadows the idealistic Renaissance
humanism to which Hamlet gives voice in his speech glorifying
'This most excellent canopy, the air . . . this brave o'erhanging
firmament, this majestical roof fretted with golden fire' and
exclaiming ecstatically on the virtues of its principal tenant,
man:

What a piece of work is a man, how noble in reason, how infinite
in faculties, in form and moving how express and admirable, in
action how like an angel, in apprehension how like a god: the

beauty of the world, the paragon of animals!

(Hamlet, II.2.299–307)

Hamlet's optimism, however, is contained syntactically within a structure which turns it to dust and ashes. He admits that he has, why he does not know, lost all his 'mirth' and 'forgone all custom of exercises'; the earth has become to him 'a sterile promontory', and the splendid features quoted above out of context are cited only to be reduced to 'a foul and pestilent congregation of vapours'. And exalted man sinks to the level of a 'quintessence of dust'. Hamlet is himself conscious that his melancholy poisons his vision; and we as audiences of the play become aware of a still wider, defiling context in which we see the Renaissance prince embroiled, and by which he is compromised, till the heroic ideal, to which he is symbolically the heir, functions more as a disillusioning contrast with reality than an affirmation. It defines what is in terms of what has been lost, and gathers to itself an overwhelming sense of corruption and degradation. Yet out of that context, Hamlet and even, to some extent, those like Claudius and Polonius who seem to be the merest agents of corruption, ultimately emerge as more recognisable, and compelling, images of the flawed human condition to which we all belong.

The Merchant of Venice is not, of course, a tragedy like *Hamlet*. There are figures such as Antonio and Shylock who are potentially tragic, but the play, despite its tragic overtones, remains within the genre of comedy, where conflicts are resolved and the traditionally happy ending signifies the triumph of life-affirming forces. Lorenzo's speech forms part of an orchestrated sequence which is designed to change the dramatic atmosphere after the acute tension of the trial scene. He and his young wife, Jessica, engage in a romantic dialogue which calls upon the resources of classical myth, saturating their poetry with tender sentiment and creating a moon-drenched series of famous nights of love to which their own elopement is seen as a modern addition. Music — that great Shakespearean theatrical resource — is also brought into play to add its 'touches of sweet harmony', culminating in Lorenzo's music of the spheres. But the fallen world has its place even here, in that the mortal limitations of time-ridden humanity inhabiting the real world, though they do not reduce the ideal to corruption as in *Hamlet,* nonetheless constitute a barrier between the ideal and the real. The very defects that make human beings their distinctively human selves, also frustrate their longings for that ultra-human harmony which imagination creates for them. For the moment the comedy seems to float romantically free from the grossness of unregenerate humanity, but in the very act of its spiritual aspiration it is brought down to earth again and closed in by 'this muddy vesture of decay' which is the fallible body.

On closer inspection this scene of myth, moonlight and music also reveals disturbing undertones. Its lyrical eloquence is at odds with the, as it were, offstage implications of the famous love exemplars it calls upon: Cressida (as satirically portrayed in Shakespeare's *Troilus and Cressida*) becomes a notorious example of unfaithfulness; Thisbe and her lover Pyramus commit suicide (as *A Midsummer Night's Dream*, though in farcical mode, demonstrates); Dido also commits suicide after being deserted by Aeneas; and, most sinister of all, Medea, though she is here remembered as the enchantress who brought Jason's father, Aeson, to life, takes revenge for Jason's desertion of her by killing their children.

Medea's revival of Aeson is particularly relevant as it seems to echo Portia's 'restoration' of Antonio in the trial scene that has just been enacted before the eyes and ears of the audience in IV.1, and also recalls other allusions to the story of Jason, Medea and the Golden Fleece made earlier in the play. For example, at I.1.168–172 Bassanio refers to Portia's 'sunny locks' as being like the golden fleece and her home in Belmont as 'Colchos' strand' to which many Jasons, himself included, 'come in quest of her'; and at III.2.241, Gratiano alludes to Bassanio's success in winning Portia with the gleeful words, 'We are the Jasons, we have won the Fleece.' To the latter remark Salerio replies, 'I would you had won the fleece [with a near pun on 'fleet'] that he hath lost', referring to Antonio's losses at sea, news of which has just been brought to Bassanio. Thus linkage between the legend of the golden fleece and Bassanio's wooing of Portia extends also to Antonio's profit and loss as a Venetian merchant, with double-edged results. On the one hand, it endows

Bassanio's courtship with the associations of classical myth and suggests that the daily trade of Venice shares in the same romantic-heroic glamour; on the other, it hints that Jason and Bassanio, like the Christian merchants of Venice, are pursuing a golden fleece which is to be valued as much in financial as amorous terms. The two, in fact, become compromisingly intertwined. Bassanio owes (in both senses of the word) his opportunity of putting in a bid for Portia's hand to the financial help given by Antonio, as is made abundantly clear by the language in which he broaches the matter to his friend:

> 'Tis not unknown to you, Antonio,
> How much I have disabled mine estate
> By something showing a more swelling port
> Than my faint means would grant continuance.
> Nor do I now make moan to be abridged
> From such a noble rate; but my chief care
> Is to come fairly off from the great debts
> Wherein my time, something too prodigal,
> Hath left me gaged. To you, Antonio,
> I owe the most in money and in love,
> And from your love I have a warranty
> To unburden all my plots and purposes
> How to get clear of all the debts I owe.

(I.1.122–134)

Not to put too fine a point on it (though that, perhaps, is precisely what he does in lines 122–125), Bassanio is an aristocratic bankrupt who sees in the 'lady richly left' at Belmont (line 161) an opportunity of restoring his broken fortunes and simultaneously repaying the 'debts' he owes to Antonio. That his debts to the latter are debts of love as much as money only underlines the ambiguity of his proposal, which in the object that it aims towards, the wooing and winning of Portia's person and estate, is similarly a matter both of love and reward. He 'ventures', like a merchant, a considerable financial sum (which is also, as frequently the case with merchants, borrowed) in the hope of profiting enough to pay back the principal and retain a surplus. Which is not to say that he is merely a cynical fortune-hunter. The play gives no reason to doubt the mutual love of Portia and Bassanio; what we have to recognise is that the disinterested virtue of love is yoked to the vested interest of financial gain in a way that makes an ideally romantic purity of motive difficult to sustain.

The corollary of all this is that Antonio's business activity must also be conceded to have a romantic as well as a practical side — a point well established by the rhetoric of the play's opening words evoking the hazards to which his commercial fleet is exposed. His 'argosies' are 'Like signors and rich burghers on the flood' to which lesser ships do reverence (I.1.9–13). They are at peril of shipwreck, but the vision of that potential shipwreck is turned into eloquence by Salerio's account of it:

> And see my wealthy Andrew docked in sand,
> Vailing her high-top lower than her ribs
> To kiss her burial

while the loss of cargo becomes an almost exotic spectacle in which 'spices' are scattered 'on the stream' and 'the roaring waters' are 'enrobed' with the owner's 'silks' (I.1.27–34). This is the romance of enterprise, or 'venture' as it is called in *The Merchant of Venice*; a risk-taking that has both its positive and negative aspects. That it can be seen in such a positive light, despite the fact that it is concerned with what from the traditional point of view is a base materialistic purpose, derives from the all-or-nothing element of chance involved (lines 27–34, quoted above are immediately followed by: '. . . now worth this,/ And now worth nothing'). Antonio cannot control what the weather or pirates may do to his ships. The very act of floating them on the sea puts them at the mercy of fortune (though ultimately, in the Christian scheme of things which governs the play's philosophy, this is subordinate to divine providence); for better, for worse, they are exposed to the imperfections of a fallen world which may give their voyages, and so their melancholy owner, either a comic or a tragic outcome.

By contrast the usurer, Shylock, calculates the risks he takes — or, in a sense, does not take risks at all, but contrives 'bonds' which ensure that the sums of money he lends out come back to him with mathematically predictable gain. In the debate between Shylock and Antonio in I.3. on the subject of interest, Antonio maintains that Shylock's way is contrary to nature (and thus to the divine will) in that it is tantamount to breeding from 'barren metal' (line 131); but Shylock tries to argue that he is doing no more than the biblical Jacob did when he controlled the outcome of his agreement with Laban by causing the ewes to give birth to parti-coloured lambs. To Antonio, what Jacob served for was a 'venture' — his agreement was:

> A thing not in his power to bring to pass,
> But swayed and fashioned by the hand of heaven.
>
> (I.3.89–90)

And this is the essence of their disagreement: Shylock thinks it appropriate to control the outcome, Antonio insists that what happens must be left to God.

Formally, Antonio is in the right, and the play's structure backs him up. He risks all himself without calculation, seems to lose all in consequence, including his own life, but is rescued by miraculous intervention and ultimately achieves great gain. Formally, Shylock is in the wrong; he seeks to calculate exactly, carrying this principle to the extreme in the trial scene, but thereby bringing about his own undoing since he gets no more nor less than his absolute bond. This patterning of values is paralleled also in the caskets plot, where Morocco and Arragon respectively allow the pursuit of gain and pride in desert to mislead them in their choice, but Bassanio's willingness to 'give and hazard all he hath' brings him all things. Likewise, Jessica's elopement from the narrow regimentation of her father's household with the Christian Lorenzo becomes not only the entrance into a more liberal-minded world of carnival and romance, but also the means of her ultimately acquiring the inheritance that she seems to have renounced. Yet in the actuality of dramatic presentation what is formally endorsed becomes the target of powerful emotional criticism. Shylock himself, though presented initially as an inveterate hater of Christians, seething with resentment at the way they undercut his business (I.3.41–42), effectively exposes the inconsistency of those Christians who give vent to unthinking anti-semitic prejudice and affect to despise money-lending, yet are willing to make use of the financial service Jews such as Shylock provide. Antonio, for all his uprightness, courage and devoted friendship to Bassanio, is totally insensitive to this hypocrisy in himself and brutal enough to continue calling Shylock dog and to spit on him, and spurn him too (I.3.127–128). And, whether Shylock's 'merry' bond is offered with malice aforethought or as a genuinely friendly overture, Bassanio's suspicion of it deserves the barbed rebuke it receives from Shylock:

> O father Abram, what these Christians are,
> Whose own hard dealings teaches them suspect
> The thoughts of others!

(I.3.157–159)

Still more strikingly, Shylock's retort to Solanio and Salerio's lack of sympathy with his grief over Jessica's elopement, but concern for Antonio's commercial disasters, argues for the shared humanity of Christian and Jew in a way that quickens the audience's sense of the gulf between 'Christian example' (III.1.64) and Christian precept. Though often played in the theatre as a pathetic plea for recognition on Shylock's part, the speech is primarily a satire on the hypocrisy of Christians which points up their radical failure to live by the standards of their religion.

Needless to say, Jessica's conversion to Christianity is also flawed. Shylock's equal concern with his daughter and his ducats may justly expose him to Christian jeers (if that is not itself an oxymoron), but Jessica's concern for her jewels is not balanced by concern for her father. The spirit, of course, is comic, and no doubt an Elizabethan audience would consider a Jewish usurer's treasure fair game. What that audience might notice, however, is that the daughter insures her 'Christian' hazard with a hefty premium, leaving as little in that respect to chance as may be.

In the trial scene Shylock's refusal to take thrice the amount of his bond shows him so poisoned by malice that he denies his own financial *raison d'être* as a usurer; he becomes his own worst enemy and, in a comic mode that Ben Jonson would have understood, gets his just come-uppance. The more so in that he has just rejected the play's most eloquent plea, which is also a central statement of its Christian ideal, in the shape of Portia's 'quality of mercy' speech. This is so well known that a modern audience almost inevitably reacts to it as a somewhat isolated, set-piece aria; and it is perhaps also true that even for the original audience it must have had the character of a self-conscious verbal *tour de force*. In such a process the words that matter most may easily be overshadowed by the rhetorical brilliance that precedes them; and these crucial words I take to be the simple

> We do pray for mercy,
> And that same prayer doth teach us all to render
> The deeds of mercy.
>
> (IV.1.197–199)

'Deeds' here are implicitly opposed to words. They share with the casket scenes a preference for plain lead over showy gold and silver, and recognise plainness as the necessary accompaniment of true self-knowledge which makes man know himself as a fallen being dependent on mercy.

By common consent the forensic defeat of Shylock is a great theatrical success. It never fails to hold its audience. And that is sometimes taken to be a reason for not enquiring too closely into its own moral consistency. Likewise there is the plausible historical plea that for Elizabethan audiences Shylock's enforced conversion to Christianity would be seen as cruel only to be kind. We must not sentimentalise it by bringing to bear anachronistically modern standards. The fact remains, however, that the play goes beyond its formal commitment to conventional Christian values and in a number of places pushes its Christian audience towards a self-critical appraisal that even the histrionic brilliance of the trial scene cannot completely obscure.

To come back, then, to the point from which this essay took its departure, the 'In such a night' exchange between Lorenzo and Jessica in V.1 is the means by which Shakespeare brings about a poetic and theatrical change of key, but also one in which sinister implications sound as significant undertones. The whole of the last Act, which it introduces, continues that process, seeming to distract the audience from the disturbing elements of hatred and animosity which have surfaced in the trial scene, as the more conventional material of oaths forsworn and abandoned pledges of love (in the form of the rings) becomes the focus of attention, but keeping a sub-text of doubt. The dialogue modulates into typically teasing comic banter, yet is shaped by rhetorical repetitions which advertise their studied artificiality:

> BASSANIO   Sweet Portia,
> If you did know to whom I gave the ring,
> If you did know for whom I gave the ring,
> And would conceive for what I gave the ring,
> And how unwillingly I left the ring
> When naught would be accepted but the ring,
> You would abate the strength of your displeasure.
> PORTIA   If you had known the virtue of the ring,
> Or half her worthiness that gave the ring,
> Or your own honour to contain the ring.
> You would not then have parted with the ring.
>
> (V.1.192–202)

The banality in the contrivance of the language, like the trans-
parency of the device by which Portia and Nerissa cause their
husbands to be forsworn yet not forsworn, may be said to
distance the audience from the matter of this lovers' quarrel.
The tension here created, unlike the tension of Shylock's 'bond',
is something which the audience's privileged knowledge auto-
matically defuses (they know that Portia–Balthasar and
Nerissa–lawyer's clerk are the same persons). Yet it plays upon
a theme — marital betrayal — potentially as disruptive as
Shylock's bond, which was itself initially but a 'merry sport'.

In plot terms, the business of the rings also echoes and
contradicts the business of the bond. At the beginning of the
trial scene the Duke says to Shylock:

> . . . the world thinks, and I think so too,
> That thou but lead'st this fashion of thy malice
> To the last hour of act, and then 'tis thought
> Thou'lt show thy mercy and remorse more strange
> Than is thy strange apparent cruelty
>
> (IV.1.17–21)

But Shylock is in earnest and does not abort the tension in this
way; it is left to Portia to do that. In the rings scene it is Portia
who both builds up the 'malice' to its 'last hour of act' and
performs the theatrical volte-face by which it is converted to
comedy. The impasse in this scene is resolved by the production
of a second 'ring' which proves, in fact, to be the same as the

first; in the trial scene no second bond is produced, but Portia's interpretation of it effectively transforms it into a weapon against Shylock instead of Antonio. These similarities and differences, further heightened by the comic device of disguise which makes female male and (since on the Elizabethan stage women's roles are played by boys) male female, serve yet again to keep worlds that are superficially isolated in imaginative contact with each other.

The Merchant of Venice, then, is a play which does not merely balance commercial realism in the story of Shylock with love romance in the story of the caskets, but creates a disturbing interaction of the two. Its seemingly opposed worlds of Belmont and Venice become one by virtue of the exchange which takes place between characters from each and the echoes they afford of each other's actions and values. Not quite the same can be said of its two religious dimensions, Christian and Jewish, since the play's ruling values are those of the Christian world to which Elizabethan England itself is committed. But a process of sceptical probing takes place which at least undermines the self-satisfied certainties of the Christian, with the result that Christian and Jew no longer fit into the separate, unrelated compartments that convention assigns them. What this ultimately means is that the play's audience is faced with the consequences of its own belief in a fallen world, which entails recognising the possibility of confusing pulls in different directions. As Launcelot Gobbo expresses it in his own farcical version of the conflict between Christian and Jewish allegiances:

> To be ruled by my conscience, I should stay with the Jew my master who, God bless the mark, is a kind of devil; and to run away from the Jew, I should be ruled by the fiend, who, saving your reverence, is the devil himself.
>
> (II.2.16–20)

Despite the romantic nature of its happy ending, and despite its formal endorsement of the Christian scale of values, *The Merchant of Venice* finds that the argument does not run all one way. No one has a monopoly of truth in its essentially fallen world.

AFTERTHOUGHTS

1

Explain the importance of the opening quotation (page 95) to the argument of this essay.

2

What significance does Draper attach to the play's allusions to the legend of the Golden Fleece (pages 97–98)?

3

Do you agree that 'Formally, Antonio is in the right' (page 100)?

4

What two 'fallen' worlds is Draper comparing at the close of this essay (page 104)?

Cedric Watts

Cedric Watts is Professor of English at Sussex University, and the author of many scholarly publications.

ESSAY

Shylock, the real Jews of Venice, and Wesker's *The Merchant*

In Part 1 of this essay, I cite some historical material about Venetian Jews in Shakespeare's day; in Part 2, I discuss *The Merchant of Venice* in the light of that material; and, in Part 3, I offer a brief assessment of Arnold Wesker's play, *The Merchant*.[1]

1

Nobody expects *The Merchant of Venice*, a comedy written *circa* 1597, to offer an account of life in Venice which, in detail, is historically accurate. On the other hand, readers (or audiences) of the play may well assume that in some obvious respects the play is likely to be accurate enough. Discussions with students

---

[1] This essay uses and revises some material in my book, *Literature and Money* (Hemel Hempstead, 1990).

suggest to me that such readers may assume, for example, that in the historical Venice of the late sixteenth century, the Christians undertook the merchant venturing while the Jews were confined to money-lending; that Christians were less mercenary and more inclined to financial generosity than were Jews; and that Jews maintained a cultural separateness of a rather joyless and puritanical kind. Comparison with the facts proves salutary. Brian Pullan's scholarly study, *Rich and Poor in Renaissance Venice*, provides some crucial information.

In the play, Shylock, who clearly prefers to charge high interest rates, is angered because Antonio, by lending gratis, forces interest rates down. In fact, as Pullan shows, the Jews of Venice were subject to elaborate and often punitive controls by the authorities. Those Jews were obliged by law to maintain charitable and non-profitable banks to provide loans to needy Christians at strictly controlled low rates: five per cent to cover expenses. In order to supply such banks, Jews took to foreign trade. At a time (1590 to 1610) when many Christian merchants, finding trade too risky, preferred to invest in estates on the mainland, the Jews sent merchandise across the sea, particularly to the Turkish empire between Dalmatia and Constantinople. In some respects their risks were greater than Antonio's, for, in addition to the hazards of storm and tempest, their cargoes were subject to depredations by anti-semitic Christian pirates, among them the Knights of St John of Malta. During this period, the magistrates of Padua reported to the Venetian senate that Jewish merchants were markedly less rapacious than Christians:

> The Jew is forbidden to invest his money in anything other than merchandise, and so long as he knows that trade is progressing and multiplying he is content with smaller gains than the Christian, who wishes to invest his money in estates, houses and other real property, and is not content with a little, but develops a voracious desire for gain.[2]

Venetian Jews were confined to a ghetto and subject to many humiliating restrictions. Numerous occupations were

---

[2] Quoted in Brian Pullan's *Rich and Poor in Renaissance Venice* (Oxford, 1971), p. 555.

denied to them; they were prevented from infringing the Christian guilds' monopoly of manufacturing. They were forbidden, for instance, to become tailors or to import new clothes.

> Behind these regulations, though it was never expressly acknowledged, there probably lay the desire to deny the Jews the satisfaction of creative work, and to thrust them into a position in which they appeared to be social parasites — dealers, middlemen and moneylenders, never producers. Anti-semitism itself foists upon the Jews the characteristics it later ascribes to their innate depravity.[3]

Nevertheless, occupations which remained open to them included those of physician, printer, bookseller, greengrocer — and musician. *The Merchant of Venice* memorably suggests that Christians (but not Jews) appreciate music, and are thus attuned to the celestial harmony which lies beyond this mortal vesture. As Lorenzo lyrically explains to Jessica (the Jewess who is 'never merry' when she hears pleasant music):

> How sweet the moonlight sleeps upon this bank!
> Here will we sit and let the sounds of music
> Creep in our ears; soft stillness and the night
> Become the touches of sweet harmony.
> . . .
> There's not the smallest orb which thou beholdest
> But in his motion like an angel sings,
> Still quiring to the young-eyed cherubins;
> Such harmony is in immortal souls
> . . .
> The man that hath no music in himself,
> Nor is not moved with concord of sweet sounds,
> Is fit for treasons, stratagems, and spoils
> . . .
> Let no such man be trusted.
>
> (V.1.54–57, 60–63, 83–85, 88)

Such a treacherous man without music is clearly Shylock, who had commanded Jessica thus:

---

[3] Pullan, p. 552.

Lock up my doors; and when you hear the drum
And the vile squealing of the wry-necked fife,
Clamber not you up to the casements then
. . .
But stop my house's ears, I mean my casements;
Let not the sound of shallow foppery enter
My sober house.

(II.5.28–30, 33–35)

In the historical Venice, however, the contrasting facts were these:

> at the turn of the century, Jewish dancing masters, musicians and players were obviously sought-after by Christian pupils and audiences — as witness a licence prepared in September 1595 to authorize a Jew to enter the houses of eleven noblemen and five other persons 'to teach their children to sing, dance and play musical instruments, freely and without restraint'. Don Livio of Ferrara, a Jew resident in the Venetian Ghetto, received permission in the Carnival season to take his pupils or 'company' to dance in the houses of noblemen during the Carnivals of 1594 and 1595.[4]

Shylock has a Christian servant, Launcelot; but Patriarch Priuli had insisted in a memorandum of 1596–97 that Jews should not employ Christian servants or workmen, must not invite Christians to eat with them, and must wear yellow caps to mark them out as members of an accursed race. Yet these demeaned pariahs were nevertheless obliged to maintain charitable banks and to provide finance for the Venetian navy. Within their ghetto they still managed to organise fraternities for alms-giving, clothing the poor, lodging foreigners, and running a children's school and an academy.

In short, the myth propagated by Shakespeare (soon after the execution in London of Dr Roderigo Lopez, a victim of antisemitic prejudice)[5] offers some remarkable contrasts to the

---

[4] Pullan, p. 553.
[5] Lopez, found guilty of plotting to poison Queen Elizabeth, was executed in June 1594. The judges referred to him as 'that vile Jew'. He was almost certainly innocent. (See *Literature and Money*, pp. 53–54.)

historical truth. Probably few readers or spectators of *The Merchant of Venice* appreciate the full extent of the ironic disparity between what Shakespeare suggests and what the life of Jews in Venice actually was. The large truth that we may infer from the play is that ideology often wields myths which induce social solidarity among the majority by postulating an alien minority on whose nature is projected society's latent malice, violence and avarice.

2

Geoffrey Chaucer is famed for his 'genial humanity', but his *Prioress's Tale* seems strongly anti-semitic, for it depicts the Jews as scheming, malicious and murderous. There has long been controversy over the extent to which Shakespeare's *The Merchant of Venice* may be regarded as anti-semitic. It seems to me that in the depiction of Shylock, Shakespeare has offered a vivid and influential incarnation of what is basically a prejudicial stereotype — the Jew as ruthless money-lender. To reinforce the stereotypical association of Jews with usury and ruthlessness, the play offers a contrasting pattern in which Christians are associated with generous giving, courageously reckless ventures, brotherly and amatory emotions, and providential good fortune; just as Shylock's chilling justification of revenge has its symmetrical counterpart in Portia's famous speech on 'the quality of mercy'. Of course, one's hopes of a more tolerant presentation of Shylock are raised when he offers this self-defence:

> Hath not a Jew eyes? Hath not a Jew hands, organs, dimensions, senses, affections, passions? Fed with the same food, hurt with the same weapons, subject to the same diseases, healed by the same means, warmed and cooled by the same winter and summer as a Christian is?

> (III.1.53–58)

But these hopes are dashed when the speech modulates into a defence of bloody revenge: 'If you poison us, do we not die? And if you wrong us, shall we not revenge?' Antonio admits that he is in the habit of spitting on Shylock, spurning him and calling him a cur; but the text predominantly endorses such prejudice: Antonio is generally depicted as noble, loving and unselfish, and even Shylock's daughter condemns the Jew as mean and joyless. As a role for an accomplished actor, Shylock clearly dominates the work: distinctive in voice and idiom, possessed of a cold calculating animosity yet capable of moments of discordant pathos and harsh glee, he offers ample exercise to the expressive talents of a mature performer; yet what may result is not the subversion of stereotype but its persuasive augmentation.

Certainly, various details of the text seem repeatedly to invoke a different version of events: a version which a later and (in some respects) more humane age might welcome, for it enables Shylock to be seen more as victim and less as would-be victimiser. Such details include: Shylock's grief at his betrayal by Jessica; the harsh anti-semitic tauntings by Gratiano; the way in which Shylock is so frequently addressed in scorn as 'Jew' (even by Portia in her 'mercy' speech); and the calculating detail in which Shylock's assets are eventually commandeered by the Christians. Again, it has often been noted that the love-relationships of Bassanio and Portia and of Lorenzo and Jessica are repeatedly expressed in financial imagery and very explicitly involve the transference of wealth. Thus Jessica, about to elope with Lorenzo, says:

> Here, catch this casket; it is worth the pains.

And a few moments later:

> I will make fast the doors, and gild myself
> With some more ducats, and be with you straight.
>
> (II.6.33, 49–50)

The phrase 'gild myself' is disturbing enough, for it suggests the power of gold coins to beautify her for Lorenzo; more disturbing is the fact that in the moment of hasty elopement, she shows such pecuniary zeal; and we are reminded that this scene of amatory fugitives is also an abscondence of thieves, for Shylock is here being robbed. (The comedy of *The Merchant of Venice* often leaves an acrid aftertaste, as when we digest the scene in which Launcelot mocks his 'sand-blind' father by informing him that his son is dead.) In turn, if we consider the circumstances of

Bassanio's choice of the correct casket, we see that in one obvious respect he is the most inappropriate suitor to choose the outwardly-ugly leaden casket, since he is dressed in the expensive finery he has worn to impress and win the wealthy Portia. Portia, of course, remarks:

> . . . for you
> I would be trebled twenty times myself,
> A thousand times more fair, ten thousand times
> More rich . . .

(III.2.152–155)

Such persistent and rather distasteful commingling of the amatory with the financial partly accounts for the distinctively bittersweet tonalities of the play's love relationships. Nevertheless, though we may seek out a more congenial sub-text, the force of the dominant text is inescapable: as a distinguished critic has remarked, 'we are in danger of forgetting the real generosity, however produced, of the Christians, the real ferocity, however explained, of Shylock'.[6]

One defence of the apparent anti-semitism of Chaucer and Shakespeare is historical. An editor of *The Prioress's Tale* says:

> The tale's anti-Semitism . . . inevitably discomfits twentieth-century readers; we are forced to recognise that Chaucer was a man of his time, sharing its faults as well as its virtues.[7]

There is one obvious objection to such a defence. When Chaucer or Shakespeare appear to be saying things of which we approve, we customarily praise those authors, and not their times, for what they say. So, if Chaucer or Shakespeare appear to be saying things of which we disapprove, it is inconsistent to put the blame on their times. The feminism of *Love's Labour's Lost*, the criticisms of racism which are implicit in *Othello*, and the ruthlessly unconventional bleakness of the ending of *King Lear*: all these show that Shakespeare was not necessarily bound by convention, tradition or popular prejudice. In its vigorous complexities which have, as centre, an endorsement of the stereotype

---

[6] A D Nuttall, *A New Mimesis* (London and New York, 1983), pp. 130–131.
[7] *The Riverside Chaucer*, ed. Larry D Benson (Oxford, 1988), p. 16.

of the avaricious Jew, *The Merchant of Venice* resembles
Belmont's golden casket which, when opened, revealed a death's-
head within.

*I don't know if J is
an anti-semitist — I hope not.*

3

Arnold Wesker's play, *The Merchant* (published in 1980), attempted to redress the balance by taking salient elements of the
plot of *The Merchant of Venice* and giving them a new interpretation. The casket scene, the bond, the trial, the reversal achieved
by Portia: these remain, but Wesker has transvalued them. In
his version, Shylock, though a money-lender, is a devoted biblio-
phile and student of cultural history; Antonio is his dearest
friend. Shylock, genial and warm-hearted, is eager to lend
Antonio informally the money that he needs, but Antonio per-
suades him that the loan must be formalised legally, since the
law insists that anyone who borrows from a Jew must enter a
bond. So the stipulation of 'a pound of flesh', to be surrendered if
the loan is not repaid, is intended by Shylock and Antonio to
mock a law which denies friendship between Jew and Gentile. In
the event, when Antonio is unable to repay the loan, Shylock
and Antonio agree to become martyrs: Antonio is prepared to
die, and Shylock expects to be put to death for taking his friend's
life. (Both agree to abide by the laws of the Venetian state.)
Thanks to Portia's forensic skills, Antonio is saved; but the state
confiscates all Shylock's goods, including his beloved library. To
Antonio's grief, Shylock is now embittered and isolated.

The deep flaw in Wesker's play, it seems to me, is the 'merry
bond', which the playwright boldly attempts to take over from
Shakespeare and transform into true friendship's gesture of
protest. As Wesker's Portia says, 'A pound of flesh is a satanic
price to conceive, even as a joke.'[8] Since Antonio and Shylock
are, in this version, such intelligent friends, the lethal riskiness
of their chosen terms for the bond seems incredibly foolish. On

---

[8] Arnold Wesker, *The Journalists / The Wedding Feast / The Merchant*
(Harmondsworth, 1980), p. 252.

the one hand, they believe that the law governing loans by Jews is inhuman in its racism; on the other hand, they go to the court, ready to die, because they believe that the laws of Venice protect all the citizens, including the Jews. The contradiction seems insuperable. In *The Merchant*, Wesker has striven bravely, with much research and theatrical gusto, to transform Shakespeare's text; but the lethal bond is a knife at the heart of its dramatic plausibility.

AFTERTHOUGHTS

1

Why does Watts begin this essay by highlighting differences between Shylock and the real Venetian Jews of Shakespeare's day (pages 106–110)?

2

Do you consider *The Merchant of Venice* to be anti-semitic?

3

Do you agree with Watts's argument that authors should not be excused for repeating prejudices of their times (pages 112–113)?

4

Is it legitimate, in your view, for a writer to reinterpret the characters and/or events of another writer's work?

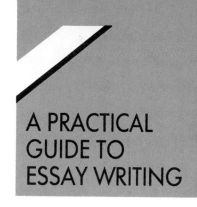

A PRACTICAL GUIDE TO ESSAY WRITING

INTRODUCTION

First, a word of warning. Good essays are the product of a creative engagement with literature. So never try to restrict your studies to what you think will be 'useful in the exam'. Ironically, you will restrict your grade potential if you do.

This doesn't mean, of course, that you should ignore the basic skills of essay writing. When you read critics, make a conscious effort to notice *how* they communicate their ideas. The guidelines that follow offer advice of a more explicit kind. But they are no substitute for practical experience. It is never easy to express ideas with clarity and precision. But the more often you tackle the problems involved and experiment to find your own voice, the more fluent you will become. So practise writing essays as often as possible.

HOW TO PLAN
AN ESSAY

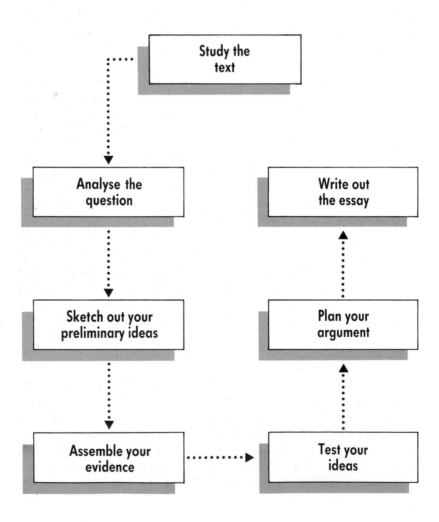

Study the text

The first step in writing a good essay is to get to know the set text well. Never write about a text until you are fully familiar with it. Even a discussion of the opening chapter of a novel, for example, should be informed by an understanding of the book as a whole. Literary texts, however, are by their very nature complex and on a first reading you are bound to miss many significant features. Re-read the book with care, if possible more than once. Look up any unfamiliar words in a good dictionary and if the text you are studying was written more than a few decades ago, consult the *Oxford English Dictionary* to find out whether the meanings of any terms have shifted in the intervening period.

Good books are difficult to put down when you first read them. But a more leisurely second or third reading gives you the opportunity to make notes on those features you find significant. An index of characters and events is often useful, particularly when studying novels with a complex plot or time scheme. The main aim, however, should be to record your *responses* to the text. By all means note, for example, striking images. But be sure to add *why* you think them striking. Similarly, record any thoughts you may have on interesting comparisons with other texts, puzzling points of characterisation, even what you take to be aesthetic blemishes. The important thing is to annotate fully and adventurously. The most seemingly idiosyncratic comment may later lead to a crucial area of discussion which you would otherwise have overlooked. It helps to have a working copy of the text in which to mark up key passages and jot down marginal comments (although obviously these practices are taboo when working with library, borrowed or valuable copies!). But keep a fuller set of notes as well and organise these under appropriate headings.

Literature does not exist in an aesthetic vacuum, however, and you should try to find out as much as possible about the context of its production and reception. It is particularly important to read other works by the same author and writings by contemporaries. At this early stage, you may want to restrict your secondary reading to those standard reference works, such as biographies, which are widely available in public libraries. In the long run, however, it pays to read as wide a range of critical studies as possible.

Some students, and tutors, worry that such studies may stifle the development of any truly personal response. But this won't happen if you are alert to the danger and read critically. After all, you wouldn't passively accept what a stranger told you in conversation. The fact that a critic's views are in print does not necessarily make them any more authoritative (as a glance at the review pages of the *TLS* and *London Review of Books* will reveal). So question the views you find: 'Does this critic's interpretation agree with mine and where do we part company?' 'Can it be right to try and restrict this text's meanings to those found by its author or first audience?' 'Doesn't this passage treat a theatrical text as though it were a novel?' Often it is views which you reject which prove most valuable since they challenge you to articulate your own position with greater clarity. Be sure to keep careful notes on what the critic wrote, and your *reactions* to what the critic wrote.

Analyse the question

You cannot begin to answer a question until you understand what task it is you have been asked to perform. Recast the question in your own words and reconstruct the line of reasoning which lies behind it. Where there is a choice of topics, try to choose the one for which you are best prepared. It would, for example, be unwise to tackle 'How far do you agree that in *Paradise Lost* Milton transformed the epic models he inherited from ancient Greece and Rome?' without a working knowledge of Homer and Virgil (or *Paradise Lost* for that matter!). If you do not already know the works of these authors, the question should spur you on to read more widely — or discourage you from attempting it at all. The scope of an essay, however, is not always so obvious and you must remain alert to the implied demands of each question. How could you possibly 'Consider the view that *Wuthering Heights* transcends the conventions of the Gothic novel' without reference to at least some of those works which, the question suggests, have *not* transcended Gothic conventions?

When you have decided on a topic, analyse the terms of the question itself. Sometimes these self-evidently require careful definition: *tragedy* and *irony*, for example, are notoriously difficult concepts to pin down and you will probably need to consult a good dictionary of literary terms. Don't ignore, however, those seemingly innocuous phrases which often smuggle in significant assumptions. 'Does Macbeth lack the nobility of the true tragic hero?' obviously invites you to discuss nobility and the nature of the tragic hero. But what of 'lack' and 'true' — do they suggest that the play would be improved had Shakespeare depicted Macbeth in a different manner? or that tragedy is superior to other forms of drama? Remember that you are not expected meekly to agree with the assumptions implicit in the question. Some questions are deliberately provocative in order to stimulate an engaged response. Don't be afraid to take up the challenge.

Sketch out your preliminary ideas

'Which comes first, the evidence or the answer?' is one of those chicken and egg questions. How can you form a view without inspecting the evidence? But how can you know which evidence is relevant without some idea of what it is you are looking for? In practice the mind reviews evidence and formulates preliminary theories or hypotheses at one and the same time, although for the sake of clarity we have separated out the processes. Remember that these early ideas are only there to get you started. You *expect* to modify them in the light of the evidence you uncover. Your initial hypothesis may be an instinctive 'gut-reaction'. Or you may find that you prefer to 'sleep on the problem', allowing ideas to gell over a period of time. Don't worry in either case. The mind is quite capable of processing a vast amount of accumulated evidence, the product of previous reading and thought, and reaching sophisticated intuitive judgements. Eventually, however, you are going to have to think carefully through any ideas you arrive at by such intuitive processes. Are they logical? Do they take account of all the relevant factors? Do they fully answer the question set? Are there any obvious reasons to qualify or abandon them?

Assemble your evidence

Now is the time to return to the text and re-read it with the question and your working hypothesis firmly in mind. Many of the notes you have already made are likely to be useful, but assess the precise relevance of this material and make notes on any new evidence you discover. The important thing is to cast your net widely and take into account points which tend to undermine your case as well as those that support it. As always, ensure that your notes are full, accurate, and reflect your own critical judgements.

You may well need to go outside the text if you are to do full justice to the question. If you think that the 'Oedipus complex' may be relevant to an answer on *Hamlet* then read Freud and a balanced selection of those critics who have discussed the appropriateness of applying psychoanalytical theories to the interpretation of literature. Their views can most easily be tracked down by consulting the annotated bibliographies held by most major libraries (and don't be afraid to ask a librarian for help in finding and using these). Remember that you go to works of criticism not only to obtain information but to stimulate you into clarifying your own position. And that since life is short and many critical studies are long, judicious use of a book's index and/or contents list is not to be scorned. You can save yourself a great deal of future labour if you carefully record full bibliographic details at this stage.

Once you have collected the evidence, organise it coherently. Sort the detailed points into related groups and identify the quotations which support these. You must also assess the relative importance of each point, for in an essay of limited length it is essential to establish a firm set of priorities, exploring some ideas in depth while discarding or subordinating others.

Test your ideas

As we stressed earlier, a hypothesis is only a proposal, and one that you fully expect to modify. Review it with the evidence before you. Do you really still believe in it? It would be surprising if you did not want to modify it in some way. If you cannot see any problems, others may. Try discussing your ideas with friends and relatives. Raise them in class discussions. Your tutor is certain to welcome your initiative. The critical process is essentially collaborative and there is absolutely no reason why you should not listen to and benefit from the views of others. Similarly, you should feel free to test your ideas against the theories put forward in academic journals and books. But do not just borrow what you find. Critically analyse the views on offer and, where appropriate, integrate them into your own pattern of thought. You must, of course, give full acknowledgement to the sources of such views.

Do not despair if you find you have to abandon or modify significantly your initial position. The fact that you are prepared to do so is a mark of intellectual integrity. Dogmatism is never an academic virtue and many of the best essays explore the *process* of scholarly enquiry rather than simply record its results.

Plan your argument

Once you have more or less decided on your attitude to the question (for an answer is never really 'finalised') you have to present your case in the most persuasive manner. In order to do this you must avoid meandering from point to point and instead produce an organised argument — a structured flow of ideas and supporting evidence, leading logically to a conclusion which fully answers the question. Never begin to write until you have produced an outline of your argument.

You may find it easiest to begin by sketching out its main stage as a flow chart or some other form of visual presentation. But eventually you should produce a list of paragraph topics. The paragraph is the conventional written demarcation for a unit of thought and you can outline an argument quite simply by briefly summarising the substance of each paragraph and then checking that these points (you may remember your English teacher referring to them as topic sentences) really do follow a coherent order. Later you will be able to elaborate on each topic, illustrating and qualifying it as you go along. But you will find this far easier to do if you possess from the outset a clear map of where you are heading.

All questions require some form of an argument. Even so-called 'descriptive' questions *imply* the need for an argument. An adequate answer to the request to 'Outline the role of Iago in *Othello*' would do far more than simply list his appearances on stage. It would at the very least attempt to provide some *explanation* for his actions — is he, for example, a representative stage 'Machiavel'? an example of pure evil, 'motiveless malignity'? or a realistic study of a tormented personality reacting to identifiable social and psychological pressures?

Your conclusion ought to address the terms of the question. It may seem obvious, but 'how far do you agree', 'evaluate', 'consider', 'discuss', etc, are *not* interchangeable formulas and your conclusion must take account of the precise wording of the question. If asked 'How far do you agree?', the concluding paragraph of your essay really should state whether you are in complete agreement, total disagreement, or, more likely, partial agreement. Each preceding paragraph should have a clear justification for its existence and help to clarify the reasoning which underlies your conclusion. If you find that a paragraph serves no good purpose (perhaps merely summarising the plot), do not hesitate to discard it.

The arrangement of the paragraphs, the overall strategy of the argument, can vary. One possible pattern is dialectical: present the arguments in favour of one point of view (**thesis**); then turn to counter-arguments or to a rival interpretation (**antithesis**); finally evaluate the competing claims and arrive at your own conclusion (**synthesis**). You may, on the other hand, feel so convinced of the merits of one particular case that you wish to devote your entire essay to arguing that viewpoint persuasively (although it is always desirable to indicate, however briefly, that you are aware of alternative, if flawed, positions). As the essays contained in this volume demonstrate, there are many other possible strategies. Try to adopt the one which will most comfortably accommodate the demands of the question and allow you to express your thoughts with the greatest possible clarity.

Be careful, however, not to apply abstract formulas in a mechanical manner. It is true that you should be careful to define your terms. It is *not* true that every essay should begin with 'The dictionary defines *x* as . . .'. In fact, definitions are often best left until an appropriate moment for their introduction arrives. Similarly every essay should have a beginning, middle and end. But it does not follow that in your opening paragraph you should announce an intention to write an essay, or that in your concluding paragraph you need to signal an imminent desire to put down your pen. The old adages are often useful reminders of what constitutes good practice, but they must be interpreted intelligently.

Write out the essay

Once you have developed a coherent argument you should aim to communicate it in the most effective manner possible. Make certain you clearly identify yourself, and the question you are answering. Ideally, type your answer, or at least ensure your handwriting is legible and that you leave sufficient space for your tutor's comments. Careless presentation merely distracts from the force of your argument. Errors of grammar, syntax and spelling are far more serious. At best they are an irritating blemish, particularly in the work of a student who should be sensitive to the nuances of language. At worst, they seriously confuse the sense of your argument. If you are aware that you have stylistic problems of this kind, ask your tutor for advice at the earliest opportunity. Everyone, however, is liable to commit the occasional howler. The only remedy is to give yourself plenty of time in which to proof read your manuscript (often reading it aloud is helpful) before submitting it.

Language, however, is not only an instrument of communication; it is also an instrument of thought. If you want to think clearly and precisely you should strive for a clear, precise prose style. Keep your sentences short and direct. Use modern, straightforward English wherever possible. Avoid repetition, clichés and wordiness. Beware of generalisations, simplifications, and overstatements. Orwell analysed the relationship between stylistic vice and muddled thought in his essay 'Politics and the English Language' (1946) — it remains essential reading (and is still readily available in volume 4 of the Penguin *Collected Essays, Journalism and Letters*). Generalisations, for example, are always dangerous. They are rarely true and tend to suppress the individuality of the texts in question. A remark such as 'Keats always employs sensuous language in his poetry' is not only fatuous (what, after all, does it mean? is *every* word he wrote equally 'sensuous'?) but tends to obscure interesting distinctions which could otherwise be made between, say, the descriptions in the 'Ode on a Grecian Urn' and those in 'To Autumn'.

The intelligent use of quotations can help you make your points with greater clarity. Don't sprinkle them throughout your essay without good reason. There is no need, for example, to use them to support uncontentious statements of fact. 'Macbeth murdered Duncan' does not require textual evidence (unless you wish to dispute Thurber's brilliant parody, 'The Great Macbeth Murder Mystery', which reveals Lady Macbeth's father as the culprit!). Quotations should be included, however, when they are necessary to support your case. The proposition that Macbeth's imaginative powers wither after he has killed his king would certainly require extensive quotation: you would almost certainly want to analyse key passages from both before and after the murder (perhaps his first and last soliloquies?). The key word here is 'analyse'. Quotations cannot make your points on their own. It is up to you to demonstrate their relevance and clearly explain to your readers *why* you want them to focus on the passage you have selected.

Most of the academic conventions which govern the presentation of essays are set out briefly in the style sheet below. The question of gender, however, requires fuller discussion. More than half the population of the world is female. Yet many writers still refer to an undifferentiated *man*kind. Or write of the author and *his* public. We do not think that this convention has much to recommend it. At the very least, it runs the risk of introducing unintended sexist attitudes. And at times leads to such patent absurdities as 'Cleopatra's final speech asserts *man*'s true nobility'. With a little thought, you can normally find ways of expressing yourself which do not suggest that the typical author, critic or reader is male. Often you can simply use plural forms, which is probably a more elegant solution than relying on such awkward formulations as 's/he' or 'he and she'. You should also try to avoid distinguishing between male and female authors on the basis of forenames. Why *Jane* Austen and not *George* Byron? Refer to all authors by their last names unless there is some good reason not to. Where there may otherwise be confusion, say between T S and George Eliot, give the name in full when it first occurs and thereafter use the last name only.

Finally, keep your audience firmly in mind. Tutors and examiners are interested in understanding your conclusions and the processes by which you arrived at them. They are not interested in reading a potted version of a book they already know. **So don't pad out your work with plot summary.**

Hints for examinations

In an examination you should go through exactly the same processes as you would for the preparation of a term essay. The only difference lies in the fact that some of the stages will have had to take place before you enter the examination room. This should not bother you unduly. Examiners are bound to avoid the merely eccentric when they come to formulate papers and if you have read widely and thought deeply about the central issues raised by your set texts you can be confident you will have sufficient material to answer the majority of questions sensibly.

The fact that examinations impose strict time limits makes it *more* rather than less important that you plan carefully. There really is no point in floundering into an answer without any idea of where you are going, particularly when there will not be time to recover from the initial error.

Before you begin to answer any question at all, study the entire paper with care. Check that you understand the rubric and know how many questions you have to answer and whether any are compulsory. It may be comforting to spot a title you feel confident of answering well, but don't rush to tackle it: read *all* the questions before deciding which *combination* will allow you to display your abilities to the fullest advantage. Once you have made your choice, analyse each question, sketch out your ideas, assemble the evidence, review your initial hypothesis, plan your argument, *before* trying to write out an answer. And make notes at each stage: not only will these help you arrive at a sensible conclusion, but examiners are impressed by evidence of careful thought.

Plan your time as well as your answers. If you have practised writing timed essays as part of your revision, you should not find this too difficult. There can be a temptation to allocate extra time to the questions you know you can answer well; but this is always a short-sighted policy. You will find yourself left to face a question which would in any event have given you difficulty without even the time to give it serious thought. It is, moreover, easier to gain marks at the lower end of the scale than at the upper, and you will never compensate for one poor answer by further polishing two satisfactory answers. Try to leave some time at the end of the examination to re-read your answers and correct any obvious errors. If the worst comes to the worst and you run short of time, don't just keep writing until you are forced to break off in mid-paragraph. It is far better to provide for the examiner a set of notes which indicate the overall direction of your argument.

Good luck — but if you prepare for the examination conscientiously and tackle the paper in a methodical manner, you won't need it!

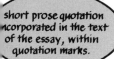

short prose quotation incorporated in the text of the essay, within quotation marks.

Three dots (ellipsis) indicate where words or phrases have been cut from quotation or where (as here) a quotation begins mid-sentence.

long verse quotation indented and introduced by a colon. No quotation marks are needed.

Line reference given directly after the quotation, in brackets.

book/play titles are given in italics. In a handwritten or typed manuscript this would appear as underlining: King Lear; Othello.

Short verse quotation incorporated in the text of the essay within quotation marks. If the quotation ran on into a second line of poetry, this would be indicated by a slash (/).

deceiving Benedick and Beatrice into 'a mountain of affection th'one with th'other' (II.1.339–340). The basis of both plots is getting the victims to overhear other people speaking, as they think, honestly.

In fact, therefore, we are being presented with two types of deceit: that which is benevolent, like Don Pedro's or the Friar's, seeking ultimately a harmony that can be expressed marriage, and that which is totally destructive, like Don J The success of each type of deceit depends on a manipul language and an alteration of behaviour and appearances on the readiness of the victims to judge from what is pres their eyes and ears. Telling the two types apart may ult.

t is not as if any character is unaware of the diff ionship of appearance to reality: but nearly every one s led hoose, of two alternatives, the wrong one. The best in tance of this comes at the crisis of the play:

> HERO ... seemed I ever otherwise to you?
> CLAUDIO Out of thee! Seeming! I will write against it.
> You seem to me as Dian in her orb,
> As chaste as is the bud ere it be blown;
> But you are more intemperate in your blood
> Than Venus, or those pampered animals
> That rage in savage sensuality.
>
> (IV.1.53–59)

Hero's innocent use of the word 'seemed' — not 'was' — gets Claudio on the raw, for it raises the issue of behaviour versus real nature that is the cause of his torment. It triggers remarkable anticipation of Othello's tortured animal im that highlights the emotional perception of the disju between appearance and what Claudio at this point beli be reality. He could not be more wrong; and he is wrong he trusted the suspect word of Don John and what he w to see at Hero's window rather than the woman he chose to as his wife. ove must, as both Desdemona (*Othello*) and Cordelia (*King Lear*) know, depend on trust: it (or its lack) can never be *proved*. Claudio is given 'ocular proof' (*Othello* III.3.360) of Hero's apparent unchasti, just as Othello is of Desdemona's by Iago, a stage-managing and manipulating

We have divided the following information into two sections. Part A describes those rules which it is essential to master no matter what kind of essay you are writing (including examination answers). Part B sets out some of the more detailed conventions which govern the documentation of essays.

PART A: LAYOUT

Titles of texts

Titles of published books, plays (of any length), long poems, pamphlets and periodicals (including newspapers and magazines), works of classical literature, and films should be underlined: e.g. David Copperfield (novel), Twelfth Night (play), Paradise Lost (long poem), Critical Quarterly (periodical), Horace's Ars Poetica (Classical work), Apocalypse Now (film). Notice how important it is to distinguish between titles and other names. Hamlet is the play; Hamlet the prince. Wuthering Heights is the novel; Wuthering Heights the house. Underlining is the equivalent in handwritten or typed manuscripts of printed italics. So what normally appears in this volume as *Othello* would be written as Othello in your essay.

Titles of articles, essays, short stories, short poems, songs, chapters of books, speeches, and newspaper articles are enclosed in quotation marks; e.g. 'The Flea' (short poem), 'The Prussian Officer' (short story), 'Middleton's Chess Strategies' (article), 'Thatcher Defects!' (newspaper headline).

Exceptions: Underlining titles or placing them within quotation marks does not apply to sacred writings (e.g. Bible, Koran, Old Testament, Gospels) or parts of a book (e.g. Preface, Introduction, Appendix).

It is generally incorrect to place quotation marks around a title of a published book which you have underlined. The exception is 'titles within titles': e.g. 'Vanity Fair': A Critical Study (title of a book about *Vanity Fair*).

Quotations

Short verse quotations of a single line or part of a line should be incorporated within quotation marks as part of the running text of your essay. Quotations of two or three lines of verse are treated in the same way, with line endings indicated by a slash(/). For example:

1   In Julius Caesar, Antony says of Brutus, 'This was the noblest Roman of them all'.

2   The opening of Antony's famous funeral oration, 'Friends, Romans, Countrymen, lend me your ears;/ I come to bury Caesar not to praise him', is a carefully controlled piece of rhetoric.

Longer verse quotations of more than three lines should be indented from the main body of the text and introduced in most cases with a colon. Do not enclose indented quotations within quotation marks. For example:

It is worth pausing to consider the reasons Brutus gives to justify his decision to assassinate Caesar:

> It must be by his death; and for my part,
> I know no personal cause to spurn at him,
> But for the general. He would be crowned.
> How might that change his nature, there's the question.

At first glance his rationale may appear logical . . .

Prose quotations of less than three lines should be incorporated in the text of the essay, within quotation marks. Longer prose quotations should be indented and the quotation marks omitted. For example:

1   Before his downfall, Caesar rules with an iron hand. His political opponents, the Tribunes Marullus and Flavius, are 'put to silence' for the trivial offence of 'pulling scarfs off Caesar's image'.

2   It is interesting to note the rhetorical structure of Brutus's Forum speech:

> Romans, countrymen, and lovers, hear me for my cause, and be silent that you may hear. Believe me for my honour, and have respect to mine honour that you may believe. Censure me in your wisdom, and awake your senses, that you may the better judge.

Tenses: When you are relating the events that occur within a work of fiction or describing the author's technique, it is the convention to use the present tense. Even though Orwell published *Animal Farm* in 1945, the book *describes* the animals' seizure of Manor Farm. Similarly, Macbeth always *murders* Duncan, despite the passage of time.

PART B: DOCUMENTATION

When quoting from verse of more than twenty lines, provide line references: e.g. In 'Upon Appleton House' Marvell's mower moves 'With whistling scythe and elbow strong' (1.393).

Quotations from plays should be identified by act, scene and line references: e.g. Prospero, in Shakespeare's The Tempest, refers to Caliban as 'A devil, a born devil' (IV.1.188). (i.e. Act 4. Scene 1. Line 188).

Quotations from prose works should provide a chapter reference and, where appropriate, a page reference.

Bibliographies should list full details of all sources consulted. The way in which they are presented varies, but one standard format is as follows:

1 Books and articles are listed in alphabetical order by the author's last name. Initials are placed after the surname.
2 If you are referring to a chapter or article within a larger work, you list it by reference to the author of the article or chapter, not the editor (although the editor is also named in the reference).
3 Give (in parentheses) the place and date of publication, e.g. (London, 1962). These details can be found within the book itself. Here are some examples:

> Brockbank, J.P., 'Shakespeare's Histories, English and Roman', in Ricks, C. (ed.) English Drama to 1710 (Sphere History of Literature in the English Language) (London, 1971).
> Gurr, A., 'Richard III and the Democratic Process', Essays in Criticism 24 (1974), pp. 39–47.
> Spivack, B., Shakespeare and the Allegory of Evil (New York, 1958).

Footnotes: In general, try to avoid using footnotes and build your references into the body of the essay wherever possible. When you do use them give the full bibliographic reference to a work in the first instance and then use a short title: e.g. See K. Smidt, <u>Unconformities in Shakespeare's History Plays</u> (London, 1982), pp. 43–47 becomes Smidt (pp. 43–47) thereafter. Do not use terms such as 'ibid.' or 'op. cit.' unless you are absolutely sure of their meaning.

There is a principle behind all this seeming pedantry. The reader ought to be able to find and check your references and quotations as quickly and easily as possible. Give additional information, such as canto or volume number whenever you think it will assist your reader.

bluespeaker
mudint
inscvperiovs
brainfart
bathos in style

SUGGESTIONS FOR FURTHER READING

Texts
Penguin Shakespeare, ed. G B Harrison (Harmondsworth, 1937); Arden Shakespeare, ed. J Russel Brown (London, 1955); and New Cambridge Shakespeare, ed. M M Mahood (Cambridge, 1987)

General Studies (containing substantial discussions of *The Merchant of Venice*)
Dessen, A C, 'The Elizabethan Stage Jew and the Christian Example', *Modern Language Quarterly*, 35 (1974)

Hattaway, M, *Elizabethan Popular Theatre: Plays in Performance* (London, 1982)

Holderness, G, Potter, N and Turner, J, *Shakespeare: the Play of History* (London, 1988)

Studies of *The Merchant of Venice*
Bulman, J C, *Shakespeare in Performance: 'The Merchant of Venice'* (Manchester, 1991)

Cohen, W, '*The Merchant of Venice* and the possibilities of historical criticism', *English Literary History*, 49 (1982)

Danson, Lawrence, *The Harmonies of 'The Merchant of Venice'* (New Haven, 1978)

Overton, B, *Text and Performance: 'The Merchant of Venice'* (London, 1987)

Wilders, J (ed.), '*The Merchant of Venice*': Macmillan Casebook (London, 1969). See especially essays by Bradbrook, Barber and Auden

Longman Group UK Limited
*Longman House, Burnt Mill, Harlow, Essex, CM20 2JE, England
and Associated Companies throughout the World.*

First published 1992
ISBN 0 582 07575 0

*Set in 10/12 pt Century Schoolbook, Linotron 202
Printed by Longman Singapore Publishers Pte Ltd
Printed in Singapore*

Acknowledgement
The editors would like to thank Zachary Leader for his assistance with
the style sheet.